It's an Old Pennsylvania Custom

EDWIN VALENTINE MITCHELL

Author of "It's an Old New England Custom"

BONANZA BOOKS, INC. • NEW YORK

Copyright, © MCMXLVII, by Edwin Valentine Mitchell

Manufactured in the United States of America

This edition published by Bonanza Books,
a division of Crown Publishers, Inc.
by arrangement with The Vanguard Press, Inc.

B   C   D   E   F   G   H

For Terry

ACKNOWLEDGMENTS

Grateful acknowledgment is made to Barrows Mussey for his help in writing this book, particularly for his many suggestions and the loan of rare books about Pennsylvania. I am also deeply indebted to Melvin Evans, whose knowledge of the state is extensive and peculiar, and to F. Ivor D. Avellino of the American History Room of the New York Public Library. My thanks are also due Mrs. Sara Sheppard Landis, Mrs. Ida Bailey Allen, Miss Nada Kramer, Mrs. Esther Reist, and Miss Reisie Lonette. I am likewise under obligation to James Thrall Soby and Theodore A. Phillips.

E. V. M.

CONTENTS

IT'S AN OLD
PENNSYLVANIA CUSTOM

BECAUSE of the housing shortage at Philadelphia and vicinity many of the early Pennsylvania settlers became cave dwellers. Both the Swedes and the English burrowed into the banks of the Delaware and Schuylkill Rivers, either enlarging natural caves or creating new artificial ones. In this they are thought to have copied the Indians, who in turn are supposed to have taken the idea from the muskrats. In any case, the first English settlers who arrived on the *John and Sarah* late in 1681 wintered in the caves beneath the high bluffs along the Delaware. The following year it was estimated that a third of the population of Philadelphia was living underground.

Some of the caves were made by digging into the ground near the edge of the river bank to a depth of three or four feet and then building a wall of earth a yard high around the excavation, thus forming a chamber half below and half above ground. The roofs were constructed of layers of limbs or split sections of trees covered with sod or bark, or thatched with straw or river rushes. The stone chimneys were laid up in mortar made of clay mixed with pebbles or reeds. Although the first English women to arrive were unaccustomed to hard labor, they nevertheless pitched in and helped their husbands, often handling one end of a saw or lovingly carrying the hod.

One Quaker lady, who became overwearied fetching water for her husband to make mortar with which to build their chimney, was requested by him to forbear. "Thou, my dear," he said gently, "had better think of dinner."

The poor woman walked away toward their tent, weeping as she went, because she did not know where their dinner was coming from. All their provisions had been exhausted, save for a small quantity of crackers and cheese, and she had not told her husband. Overwrought and homesick, she blamed herself for coming here to be exposed to such hardships. While in this low state of mind, she suddenly felt herself reproved, as if she were being queried with, "Didst thou not come for liberty of conscience? Hast thou not got it? Also been provided for beyond thy expectations?" This so humbled her that she fell on her knees and asked forgiveness, promising never to repine again.

When she arose and was about to seek other food among her friends, her cat walked into the tent with a fine large rabbit which it had caught. Gratefully receiving what the cat brought in, she dressed and jugged it as an English hare. When at dinner she told her husband the facts, it is related that they both wept with reverential joy and, in singleness of heart, ate the meal which had been thus seasonably provided.

The first child born of English parents in Philadelphia came into being in one of the waterfront caves near Penny Pot landing, so called from a tavern of that name. This cave child was John Key, who was nicknamed the First Born. In 1713, when he was thirty-one years old, William Penn honored him with the gift of a lot of land on the south side of Sassafras Street, which Key kept for a couple of years and then sold for twelve pounds. Breathing the imprisoned air of a cave in babyhood apparently had no ill effects on the First Born, for he lived to be immensely old. He died at Kennet in Chester County, July 5, 1767, at the age of eighty-five, and was interred the following day in the Quaker burial ground there in the presence of a great concourse of people. Within a few years of his death he thought nothing of walking from Kennet to Philadelphia, a distance of about thirty miles, in a single day.

Oddly enough, on August 10 of that same year there died at Brandywine Hundred the first-born child of English parents in the *province*, one Emanuel Grubb, who was born in 1681, a year before John Key. This venerable man of eighty-six was active and vigorous to the last, actually riding his horse to Philadelphia and back, a total distance of some forty-odd miles, only a few months before his death.

It is only fair to state that there is a contender for the title of First Born. Edward Drinker, the son of Quaker parents, was born in a log cabin within the future limits of Philadelphia two years before William Penn's arrival. This would make him older than either Key or Grubb, and he may well be the rightful claimant and the other two just pretenders. Anyway, he outlived them both.

Although cave dwelling was apparently not harmful to the health of the populace, it did have a bad effect on the morals of some of the persons clus-

tered in these darksome dens. In 1685, the grand
jury presented Joseph Knight for suffering drunken-
ness and evil orders in his cavern, and on representa-
tion of the Philadelphia magistrates all families
living in caves were ordered to appear before the
Provincial Executive Council. What a motley procession of underworld characters this would have
made. But no one paid any attention to the order,
even though it was backed by a letter from William
Penn. Empty caves within the line of Front Street,
however, were ordered demolished and were filled
in. But the bulk of the caves remained intact, and
were in use for at least the first half century of
Philadelphia's history.

On the whole, the denizens of the caves were not
a carousing, wanton set, but pious, honest, decent
folk. In 1683, the distinguished and learned German
colonist, Francis Daniel Pastorius, the founder of
Germantown, landed at Philadelphia with a few
followers and took temporary quarters in a cave,
wherein he lived "more contentedly than many
nowadays in their painted and wainscoted palaces."
It was in his subterranean abode overlooking the
Delaware that lots were cast for plots in the Germantown tract which Pastorius had purchased for himself and for others from William Penn.

Ten years after Pastorius and his colleagues had
settled Germantown, a most extraordinary com-

pany of men appeared there. This strange band was a parcel of hermits, fifty mystical German monks, Brothers of the Society of the Woman in the Wilderness, who had chosen Germantown for their retreat. Under the leadership of John Kelpius they established themselves along the darkly wooded ravine of Wissahickon Creek, where they built log huts and hollowed out caves for their hermitages. A small natural grotto in the hillside, the entrance to which was overshadowed by giant pines and hemlocks and near which was a spring of pure water, was reserved by the brotherhood for their leader. In this romantic hermit den, Kelpius, "maddest of good men," as Whittier described him, "dreamed o'er the Chiliast dreams of Petersen."

How did these Hermits of the Wissahickon, as they came to be called, come by the curious name of their order, Brothers of the Society of the Woman in the Wilderness? In the Book of Revelation the mysterious woman is referred to as coming out of the wilderness leaning on her beloved. It may be that Kelpius and his disciples looked forward to meeting her, though she seems rather to have symbolized and foreshadowed the approaching millennium or the great deliverance they believed to be in store for them. Since the revelations which they deemed imminent could not be imparted in the turmoil and wickedness of the world, but only in the solitude and tranquility of the wilderness, the brothers felt that to be properly prepared to receive them they should live apart in detached discomfort.

The Hermits of the Wissahickon, among whom were many men of education and several excellent musicians, waited patiently for a decade for something to happen, but nothing did, until suddenly Kelpius died. He was only thirty-four at the time and was preaching to his followers in his garden when the end came. As in the case of many other religious communities, the loss of the leader proved a fatal blow to the colony. There were dissensions over the question of celibacy. Love made inroads in the band by claiming a number of hermits. Loneliness caused others to enter holy wedlock, but none of the wives became hermitesses, and the married hermits drifted away. With Kelpius gone, there was no one to hold the remaining brothers together, and the Society of the Woman in the Wilderness gradually disintegrated. Today Hermit Lane in Germantown commemorates this unique colony of cave-dwelling hermits.

Pennsylvania has had other hermits besides these German Pietists. Very famous in his day was Amos Wilson, the Pennsylvania Hermit, who, more than a century ago, lived for nineteen years in Indian Echo Cave at Hummelstown, near Harrisburg. Wilson turned hermit when he failed by a matter of minutes to save the life of his sister, Harriot, who was hanged for murdering her illegitimate child after her lover jilted her. Provided with a pardon from the governor, Wilson hastened to the place of execution, only to find that his sister had been launched into eternity a few minutes before. This made a misanthrope of him, and he spent the remaining years of his life in the commodious limestone cave at Hummelstown, writing his commentaries on society. If you visit the cave today, you will be shown a table, a bed, and a fireplace, which it is claimed the Pennsylvania Hermit used.

None of the early settlers could possibly have guessed how rich in caves Pennsylvania would prove to be. The limestone areas of the state abound in caverns. In Centre County, for example, it is said that you can go underground at one end of the county and emerge at the other end by threading your way through the natural subway formed by the series of caverns that underlie the region. Whether this can actually be done or not is questionable, but the fact remains that the county is honeycombed with underground galleries and chambers.

About a dozen Pennsylvania caves are commercially exploited and attract thousands of visitors annually. But dozens of others are not only undeveloped, but are seldom visited, and some are still unexplored. While many caves are historically old, others are recent discoveries. Professional and amateur speleologists, specialists in cave study, find Pennsylvania a rewarding field for their activities. Exploring caves is a thrilling business of interest not only to geologists, but also to anthropologists, zoologists, and, to a lesser degree, botanists. Actually, there is a cave flora, mostly ferns and mosses, which have become used to living in perpetual darkness, after the fashion of plants that thrive without benefit of light in the dark glooms of dense tropical jungles.

Long before the days of electric torches, two youthful explorers with a queer passion for caves, who penetrated to the remoter recesses of Delaney's Cave in Laurel Hill near Uniontown, had a narrow escape when on returning they lost their way and exhausted their supply of candles trying vainly to get out. These two young men, Crain and Merrifield, who wandered about until they were completely in the dark, were resigned to their fate when they were found two days later. One of them could not speak. Some time afterward a visitor reported seeing the name Crain and the date 1802 written on the rocks in a very distant part of the cave.

The Indians used pine torches to illuminate the interiors of the caves they used. Traces of their occupancy have been found in several ancient caverns, notably Conodoguinet Cave, on the banks of the creek of that name near Carlisle, in Cumberland County, and Crystal Cave, a few miles to the westward of Kutztown, in Berks County. Bits of pottery, shells, arrowheads, and other ancient Indian implements have been discovered in these places amid the bones of four-footed beasts, birds, and serpents. Although human bones have been found in some caves, it is considered unlikely that the Indians made a practice of entombing their dead in caverns. They were more likely to use them as occasional habitations for the living, especially during the winter when a cave offered relative warmth and dryness.

As for cave worship, it is impossible to say whether the Indians of Pennsylvania practiced it or not. It is one of the most primitive forms of worship, predating the dawn of history. It is a cult of the female principle, according to Norman Douglas, a manifestation of early man's instinctive desire to hide in the womb of Mother Earth, from whom we derive our sustenance and who, when life is over, receives us. The idea is present, perhaps, in the familiar lines of a great hymn:

> Rock of Ages, cleft for me,
> Let me hide myself in thee.

Durham Cave, near the junction of Durham Creek and the Delaware River in Bucks County, was used by the notorious Catherine Montour, alias Queen Esther, the half-breed "white queen" of the Seneca Indians, on her journeys between Philadelphia and Seneca Lake, New York. The cavern chamber she occupied was called Queen Esther's room. It was ruined, as was most of the cave, when limestone was taken from the hill in which the royal cavern was situated to feed the hungry maw of Durham Furnace. Adventurers penetrating the cave reported that it measured nearly a hundred yards in length and forty feet in breadth at the widest, with a ceiling ranging from a dozen to twenty feet in height. But if one can no longer visit Queen Esther's old quarters in Durham Cave, one can still see Queen Esther's Rock in the town of Wyoming, where the bloody sacrifice of prisoners took place following the Indian and Tory attack on the Wyoming Valley settlements during the Revolutionary War. The unfortunate prisoners were ranged around the rock on which Queen Esther stood. Whirling in a kind of mad dervish dance, she tomahawked the captives one after the other, bashing their brains out against the rock, in revenge, it is said, for the loss of her son who was killed in the fight. One or two of the prisoners managed to break loose when they saw what the eccentric Queen was up to and dashed through the surrounding ranks of Indians and Tories to freedom. They were the only survivors.

Caves are great breeders of old wives' tales, and it is a pretty poor cavern that cannot produce a yarn or two. Indian legends cling like bats to the Pennsylvania caves which have been known a long time. These legends generally follow the same romantic pattern. They usually tell a tale of the love of an Indian brave for a white girl, or that of a white youth for an Indian maiden. Whether miscegenation takes place or not, the story generally ends sadly on a note of valediction and doom. Here in brief are a couple of sample legends.

Veiled Lady Cave in Centre County is so called from a white, statue-like formation within the entrance which is supposed to be the cloaked figure of a local girl named Patricia McCochran, who waited so long for her Indian lover, Strongheart, with whom she had agreed to run away, that she froze to death and turned to stone. He failed to appear because he had been mortally hurt on his way to the cave.

At nearby Penn's Cave the story is told of a Frenchman, Malachi Boyer, who had an affair with an Indian girl, Nita-nee, a chief's daughter, with whom he planned to elope. But their plans were frustrated by Nita-nee's seven brothers, who pursued the lovers and bottled Boyer up in the cave until he starved to death.

Penn's Cave, incidentally, got its name from the

fact that Penn's Creek, which was christened for Governor John Penn in 1764, rises in it. In some places at certain seasons the water in the cave is thirty-five feet deep. It never freezes, for the cave has an even year-round temperature of fifty degrees. Tourists are taken through by boat.

One of the most interesting classes of cave dwellers Pennsylvania can boast of is her criminal class. From time immemorial caves everywhere have been popularly associated with the desperadoes who have traditionally used them as hiding places for themselves and their plunder. Indeed, there is not much use in having caves if you haven't the robbers to haunt them. Since Pennsylvania is well stocked with caverns, it is pleasant to report that in the past it also had the outlaws to occupy them. Outstanding in the state's underground gallery of rogues are Simon Girty, Davy Lewis, Jim Fitzpatrick, and the Doane brothers—as fine a covey of gallows birds as anyone could desire.

Simon Girty, whose cavern retreat was in the mountains of Snyder County, was a renegade from Virginia who, in provincial days, cast in his lot with the Seneca Indians and committed many crimes. He is commemorated by a rocky profile on a cliff known as Girty's Face, which is visible from US 11 as you drive southward along the western side of the Susquehanna below Selinsgrove.

It's an Old Pennsylvania Custom

A cave near Bedford Springs in Bedford County was the headquarters of Davy Lewis, a picturesque fellow with a rather elevated moral code for a thug. He was fond of plundering the rich and making receivers of stolen goods out of the poor. In 1815 he was flung into jail as a counterfeiter, but escaped by tunneling under a wall. He released all the other prisoners before crawling out himself, with the exception of "a common fellow who had robbed a poor widow."

Another bold Pennsylvania outlaw was Jim Fitzpatrick, popularly called Fitz or Captain Fitz, who, during the winter the British were in Philadelphia and the year following, kept Chester County in a state of alarm by his daring depredations. He was a deserter from the American army who traitorously espoused the British cause. He never molested his Tory friends, but considered the Whigs only his enemies and himself at liberty to harass them in every possible manner. Like Davy Lewis, he was a social-minded robber who soaked the rich and played benefactor to the poor. The Whig collectors of public money he singled out as special objects of his vengeance. One of these collectors he not only plundered of a large sum but took off to his cave in the woods, where he kept him captive for a fortnight, until the collector's family and friends believed him murdered.

Once Fitz was pursued by a company of fifty or more armed men who were resolved to take him dead or alive. He led them a grand chase over the hills for several hours, until his pursuers became weary and stopped at a tavern for rest and refreshment. While they were taking their ease at the inn and everyone was expressing the wish to meet Fitz, he suddenly entered the room, rifle in hand. Declaring he would shoot the first man who moved, he called for a glass of rum which he tossed off and, backing out of the place, he took to his heels.

Shortly after this, when another party of eighteen or twenty men were hunting him, he stepped out from behind a tree and asked one of the company who had become separated from the others whom he was seeking.

"Fitz," answered the man.

"Then," said Fitz, "come with me and I will show you his cave where you may find him."

When he had led the man some distance from his companions, Fitz told the fellow who he was, disarmed him, and after tying him to a tree administered a severe flogging. He then told the chastened manhunter he could go and inform his comrades where they could find their quarry. But when they reached the place, Fitz had decamped.

One day after a price had been placed on his head, he walked boldly from the Southern Hill opposite

Kennett Square, through a crowd of people who made way for him, to Taylor's Tavern. Here he took a glass of grog and departed without a hand being raised against him, though there were armed men in the throng on this occasion. Fitz was fortified with a brace of pistols and a dagger.

When a man from Nottingham, a name evocative of Sherwood Forest and Robin Hood, visited Fitz's home in search of him and was rude to his mother and broke her spinning wheel, Fitz vowed vengeance. He sent word to the fellow that he would drop around to see him presently, at which the man laughed heartily and swore he would be glad to see him. But when Fitz did appear at his door and ordered him to follow him to the woods, the fellow did not have the courage to disobey. Fitz lashed him to a tree and thrashed him soundly.

Many stories are told of this daring bandit who started life as an honest enough Chester County blacksmith. His mischievous career was terminated when he was betrayed by his mistress. This miserable creature tipped off the authorities, and men concealed in her house trapped Fitz when he came from his hiding place to visit her. They took him to Chester, where he was speedily tried, condemned, and executed. He behaved throughout, we are told, with the firmness worthy of a hero.

Doane's Cave on Tohickon Creek, a mile or so

above Point Pleasant where the creek flows into the Delaware, took its name from a gang of Quaker desperadoes, the Doane brothers of Plumpstead Township, who during the Revolution did a profitable business plundering their Bucks County neighbors of horses and cattle and selling them to the British in Philadelphia. There were six boys in the Doane family, all of them distinguished for their athletic prowess. They could out-run and out-jump all competitors, and it is said that one of them, the biggest bounder of the lot, could leap over a wagon. All were professed Tories and unspeakable blackguards.

The Doanes had an organized line from Bucks County through Chester County and the Cumberland Valley into Virginia and Carolina. When the British retired, the Doanes and their confederates— Fitz was one of them—carried on an extensive trade among themselves by stealing horses in the South, passing them along the line to the North, where they could not be identified, and exchanging them for others stolen in the North. A full account of the escapades and escapes of these Bucks County bandits would make a long chronicle of crime.

At length it was learned that Moses Doane, the captain of the band, and two of his brothers were at a cabin near their cave on Tohickon Creek. A posse of men under Colonel Hart surrounded the house, but, instead of shooting the scoundrels on the spot,

Colonel Hart opened the door and cried, "Ah, you're here, are you?"

The Doanes grabbed their arms and shot down one of the posse. In the confusion, two of the brothers escaped through the back window into the woods. Moses surrendered and was promptly killed by one of the posse, who was suspected of being implicated with the Doanes. It was supposed he shot Moses on the theory that dead men tell no tales. Anyway, the other two were taken later in Chester County and hanged in Philadelphia. The rest fled to Canada, where one of them became entangled with the law and was executed.

Not all Pennsylvania caves have grim associations, nor have vandals succeeded in destroying all the beauty of these natural wonders. In some caves large numbers of stalactites have been wantonly broken off for souvenirs, but others still remain, as do many curious formations named for objects they are supposed to resemble, such as Eagle's Wings, Lobster Claws, Bunch of Bananas, Petrified Lion, and Lebanon Bologna. In a land so riddled with caves as Pennsylvania, virgin caverns are bound to be brought to light, and these may compensate for those which have been ruined.

Henry W. Shoemaker, in a paper on the caves of Centre County read at State College, told a pleasant anecdote of Stover Cave, between Aaronsburg and Pine Creek. A hundred yards inside the entrance one descends a ladder into a vast chamber. Years ago a secret society of Penn's Valley boys and girls built a dance floor here and, though most of them were for religious reasons forbidden to dance, they broke the rules. Every Saturday night mysterious music and rough folk laughter was heard issuing from the cavern as the young people tripped it to the strains of the dulcimer, the dudelsack, and the geik or fiddle. Cave life in Pennsylvania could be gay.

PENNSYLVANIA talk has created a good deal of fun for outsiders in the last two hundred years. Such things as a scrawled sign pinned on the doorpost, "Bell Don't Make, Please Bump," have been in circulation a long time. A recent volume entitled *Grandpa Is All* first mystifies the browser, then amuses him when he realizes that this is Pennsylvanian, signifying the unfortunate man's demise.

Actually there are three main sources of Pennsylvania talk, all quite unrelated, besides the everyday Philadelphia accent, which is a sort of cross, naturally enough, between Jersey and Southern drawl.

Further, there is an unmistakable Pennsylvania intonation, easily recognized when your interlocutor asks a question. Instead of asking, "Going over to Hershey tonight?" with the steadily rising inflection customary in other parts of the country, he inquires, "Going over to *Hershey* tonight?" falling back at the end.

To pick up this trick, which doesn't sound like a query at all to non-Pennsylvanians, is fatally easy and almost necessary if you want bus drivers and soda-jerkers to catch your drift the first time. Where it sprang from I don't know. I have heard it in both central and western Pennsylvania, and ascribing it to the Pennsylvania Dutch is merely a convenient way of shoving all oddities onto them. Whatever its origin, a man who talks like that might as well be tattooed with Penn's Treaty with the Indians.

The three streams of Pennsylvania speech are German, Scottish, and Quaker. All three are being whittled away fast by the march of progress, but the informed ear finds plenty of traces in idiom, vocabulary, and proper names.

The least individual, because it is spread also over Maryland and Virginia, is the Scottish. Since it is heavily Scotch-Irish, you might expect it, like Ulster

Presbyterianism, to be fiercer than the original. Actually, however, any burr you hear will probably be genuine first-generation Clydeside. Reports of "pure Elizabethan" spoken in the Cumberland mountains have often reached but never impressed me. The direct Scottish talk in Pennsylvania is limited to such phrases as the (ultimately Norse) "redding up" of a room.

What the local Scotch-Irish town officials did to personal names, on the other hand, will endure as long as there is any German stock in Pennsylvania.

German immigration to Pennsylvania began in 1683, but did not bulk large until about 1718. By that time the linguistically inept English and the inflexible Scots had settled in ahead. They kept the first records, and so forcibly imposed the first American coloration on the newcomers.

All ship captains bringing immigrants to Philadelphia were required to turn in a list of the passengers' names. After 1727 they were not only supposed to, but usually did. The immigrants themselves signed their names, if they could write, to documents swearing allegiance to the new king and forswearing any chance Roman Catholicism they might be encumbered with.

From the immigrant port of Philadelphia these people spread out into central Pennsylvania; they took undisputed possession of Berks, Lebanon, and

Lehigh counties, and overlapped into others. Some settled the Shenandoah Valley in Virginia. All told, the "Dutch country" is said to cover some 17,500 square miles.

What with the ships' captains, the oaths of allegiance, and the subsequent town records of taxation and land transfer, we have three sets of names, often covering the same people as many times. And so, as the learned, indefatigable H. L. Mencken points out, we have a fine view of what happened when the mariners, the Penns, and the town officials got in their licks.

Suppose some steerage passenger bore a name whose modern, conventional, literary German form would be Johannes Vorbach. In the first place, he probably thought of himself as Johann Vorpach. He might sign this to his oath of allegiance. What the ship's captain would list him as was anybody's guess.

Finally, when he contrived to buy a few acres of fat Susquehanna land he would face some McCullough, Carr, or Ferguson, and McCullough, Carr, or Ferguson would write the new landholder down as John Forepaugh.

Fischbach would depart rejoicing in the name of Fishpaw; Heinz and Kunz, the German counterparts of Tom, Dick, and Harry, would come out Hines and Coons. People with easier names got off easier, except that their names looked different even when they sounded the same: Reuss, Royce; Klein, Cline; Kuehle, Keeley; and Oehm emerged under the Yankee tag of Ames.

Anybody who had a *ch* in his name was out of luck. Bachmann could expect nothing better than Baughman. Albright College is named after an early divine called Albrecht. The Blochs who turned out Blacks were better off than the Hochs who became Hokes.

The fix of those with swishing names was hardly better. Schnaebele went down to posterity as Snively, Schwab as Swope, Schlosser as Slusser. What befell any Joachim Schlossbacher I leave you to imagine.

In general, whenever you see an unfamiliar or outlandish name that might by a stretch of the imagination be twisted into German pretzel shape you can safely assign its owner's family to Pennsylvania. You may not be able to trace Studebaker and Rockefeller back to their original Studebecker and Roggenfelder, but you should be able to track their footsteps from Indiana and Ohio back one step nearer the Rhine.

Occasionally the Germans would turn the tables. Any old Pennsylvania *Almanach und Kalender auf das Jahr 1820*, say, is quite likely to bear such an imprint as "Germantaun," or some small place in

"Libanon County." I have even heard of a region in Hesse, Germany, where returned immigrants brought back the verb *hellreesen, ich reese hell, wir haben hellgereest.*

The question of whether these settlers with the hard names were German or Dutch is one that troubles almost nobody except a few stickling sociologists. Occasionally a visitor from California or Texas may think the people came from Holland, but most of us are by habit closer to the old English name "Dutch" for anything beyond the Rhine. If the Germans at home will call themselves *deutsch, duetsch,* or *duitsch,* how can they resent our saying "Dutch" as our British ancestors did, not always specifying whether "high" or "low" Dutch? By the way, "high" and "low" have nothing to do with elevated style or social station; they signify high—southern —and low—northwestern—country in Germany.

In point of fact the Pennsylvania immigrants, though often poor and ignorant, were without exception "high Dutch" from southwest Germany, from Saxony, and from Switzerland. Hesse, Baden, Württemberg, and Alsace all poured in their thousands. By 1775, says Mencken, there were 90,000 Dutch. But linguistically the tone was set by the settlers from the Palatinate. Pennsylvania Dutch descends from the dialect of Westrich in that district.

I have neither the intention nor the ability to sink

this book with a learned disquisition on diphthongs, vowel changes, and inflectional decay. Having said briefly what the language is, I will merely hand on the estimate of an authority who thought, a dozen years ago, that in the three Dutch counties nearly two-thirds of the people could speak the dialect, and possibly one-third habitually did.

This is a radical change from a century back, when whole blocks of townships were solidly Dutch, and you had to hope you would be lucky in finding a stray schoolmaster who might understand your English—a condition that persisted into the eighties. I have heard, but never succeeded in tracking down, a tale to the effect that once Congress voted to decide whether English or German should be the national language, and that the deciding vote for English was cast by a Pennsylvania German. The story might have some probability if limited to Pennsylvania.

The unlucky Pennsylvania Dutch can do nothing to suit the linguists. We laugh at them for their "I went the stairs up, and looked the window out," while Heidelberg Ph.D.s used to be even more horrified by *Es giebt gar kein use, ick kann es nicht standen,* or *Mein stallion hat über die Fenz geschumpt und dem Nachbar sein whiet abscheulich gedamatscht.* Other words that stud any Pennsylvania Dutch dialogue are *affis* (where you do business), *boghie* (a vehicle), *bortsch* (not a soup, but a veranda), *ennihau,* and *gutbei* as they see you drive off down the *tornpeik.*

A parallel process began early in the German immigration with the translating rather than transliterating of names. One nineteenth-century historian declares that the proprietors ordered the settlers to translate their names into English. Whether this or a mere natural impulse was the cause, I will not undertake to decide; in either case, our identification of Pennsylvania stock two centuries after and far from home is made much harder by the great number of Carpenters who were Zimmerman, Smiths né Schmidt, Shepherds late Schaefer, Pounds out of Pfund, and Birdsongs who are fugitives from Vogelgesang.

Mencken even offers the further case of Czechs and Poles who assimilated themselves to Pennsylvania by taking German names, as a Russian family in Boston once Americanized themselves into Murphys. A Czech named Sÿr, which means cheese, thought of turning it into Käse, but then went the whole hog with Casey. Hungarian Covacses turned Schmidt are quite common, he says.

The last of the three Pennsylvania dialects (or idioms or speechways, if you must be sociological) is that of the Friends. They themselves call it Plain Speech.

Plain Speech, which perhaps I should write without capitals, to carry out the tradition, was the tongue of the Plain Friend—the man who would be called Old Broadbrim by his worldly neighbors because of his seventeenth-century hat, who wore no collar on his coat, who had breeches and wool stockings instead of pantaloons, and who thought not only dancing and drinking but singing and painting were of this world and of the Devil.

There are no true Plain Friends left, even in Westtown or Upper Merion; I doubt that any survived into this century. The tradition was strong enough at Quaker Haverford College, so that David Bispham, who later became a great concert tenor, as an undergraduate had to leave his zither with the station master off campus and to practice his arias across the railroad tracks where the college authorities could not catch him.

The same college required the young Maxfield Parrish to scrub off his room door a full-length painting of an insufficiently Plain female subject. Parrish's chemistry notebook, illustrated with watercolor elves sliding down retorts, is displayed more proudly now than it presumably was in Haverford's plainer days.

The Plain Friend, of course, was a literal follower of George Fox, who taught his people to abjure all worldly vanities. The only way he could do this was to adopt the costume and ways that were slightly backward in the mid-seventeenth century. Collars and cuffs marked the man of fashion; off with them. Presumably the Borsalinos, Stetsons, and Dunlaps of London at the time were sponsoring the narrower brim and taper crown; so Fox adopted the broad brim and round crown.

To stay three paces behind the fashion would have involved a process like that of an elderly New England spinster I knew who went to New York annually, bought a complete wardrobe at Altman's, and hung it up to cure for a year while she wore last year's purchases. The Plain Friends met this problem by anchoring themselves sartorially at 1625, bidding defiance to the passing decades.

But by 1825 they looked pretty funny. By 1875 most of them had realized that having your rather expensive tailor—the Friends have always willingly paid for quality what they would not give for style—carefully produce a fashion a quarter-millennium old showed a preoccupation with worldly things that George Fox would not have liked at all. And so another characteristic eccentricity of the eastern Pennsylvania landscape disappeared.

Speech fashions, however, are harder to shake off. Besides, people who have formed a compact religious group for three centuries need some mark to set them off, at least among themselves, from the profane. Habit and affection have kept plain speech alive.

George Fox would not fight; he would not swear, but only affirm; and he would not bestow titles and honorifics on the worldly great. He thought, rightly enough I should say, that "Friend" William was the highest title any man needed.

It took a George Fox, however, to be a true friend to all the world, and this form of address was gradually reserved for other members of the Society.

For a non-fighting man, Friend George was pretty determined. Not only would he not call peers My Lord or judges Your Honor, he would not multiply anyone's ego by calling him You.

Of course all European languages have a second person singular—*thou, tu, du*—and a second person plural—*ye, vous, ihr*. And at about the same point in early modern times they all began using the plural as a sign of respect to individuals—the inverse, no doubt, of the royal *we*. The singular was reserved for the familiarity of love, worship, or contempt. In English the objective *you* crowded out the nominative *ye*; the Germans and Danes even carried obsequiousness one step further by addressing you as *they* (*Sie, De*).

This was just the sort of thing that George Fox would have none of. By 1650, when he began the practice, calling a man *thou* meant that he was either of your own intimates or socially inferior. The judges who were constantly hauling up George Fox found themselves addressed with no civility at all, not only by name instead of title, but by the rugged, old-fashioned *thou* that properly belonged to sweeps and ostlers. Fox realized perfectly well that his life in jail was smoothed not at all by the rough outer bark of his conscience. Nevertheless, he persisted.

And hence came the plain speech of the Friends. English Quakers still say *thou*, and some Americans still write it. In general, however, the nominative *thou*, like *ye*, has succumbed to the objective *thee*. And by a process that I do not claim to understand, the third-person verb has become attached to it.

Among the Pennsylvania Friends, then, you hear the familiar form, "Thee is going to be late for Meeting. Has thee got thy umbrella?" Some Friends even say *thee* for *thy*—"Has thee got thee umbrella?" This, said an essayist, was the sacrifice of grammar on the altar of religion, forgetting that altars have no place in a Friends' meeting house.

Plain speech, like the "Friend Edward" of an earlier day, is confined now to Friends among themselves. It makes a pleasant, familiar substitute for the French conjugal and affectionate *tu*, and will probably survive as long as the Society.

That should please the shade of George Fox, but I

think he might feel that the youth of today was unduly flaming if he could overhear the excited shouts on the soccer fields of Westtown, Haverford, and Swarthmore—"Brinton, thee scoundrel, don't trip me again!" "Well, confound thee, Jones, get thy fat fanny out of the way!"

BLUEPRINTS for Utopias seldom differ greatly. One terrestrial paradise is apt to be very like another, but it is a noticeable fact that, when one of these visions solidifies and becomes a reality, its tenure of existence is usually longer when the primary motive behind it is religious rather than economic. At any rate, that has been the case in Pennsylvania, which has been the scene of more experimental colonies than any other region in America. The state is strewn with the ruins of old Utopias.

[35]

The Harmony Society was perhaps the most successful of the social experiments tried in Pennsylvania in the nineteenth century. The society migrated twice, founding three towns, and enjoyed an existence of a full century before it withered and died. It was a religiously inspired adventure, its members seeking to live after the manner of a primitive Christian community, but its worldly affairs were shrewdly administered, and the society was financially prosperous for most of its long life.

George Rapp, the leader of this communistic group, was born in Württemberg, Germany, in 1757. He was a lay preacher of peasant background, whose honesty and crusading sincerity won him numerous followers. Persecuted for their religious views and disturbed by the unsettled state of affairs in Europe, the Rappites decided to seek a haven in America. Rapp left his adherents in charge of his assistant, Frederic Reichert, and sailed for the United States in quest of a place to settle, arriving at Baltimore in the summer of 1803. Accompanied by two members of his group, he began at once to look for a site for his colony. The possibilities of several places in Maryland and Ohio were explored, but the site finally chosen was a tract of land on Connoquenessing Creek, about twenty-five miles northwest of Pittsburgh, in Butler County, Pennsylvania. Here

Rapp purchased five thousand acres of unimproved land for three dollars an acre. It was a good situation, but the region was thinly settled and still largely a wilderness. It was a place where the colonists would have to work hard to get their venture going.

Consequently, none was urged to leave the old country, but the following summer two shiploads of German emigrants, about six hundred altogether, arrived with Reichert and not long afterward began clearing the land and building homes for themselves at the place Rapp had chosen. They called the town Harmony, and their organization, which was perfected early in 1805, the Harmony Society. All property was held in common and all worked for the common interest, the welfare of each individual thus being secured. Any member who became dissatisfied and wished to detach himself from the society could get back the value of his original investment. If he had brought nothing with him, he was rewarded for his services according to the length of time he had served the society, his behavior while a member, and his immediate needs. George Rapp was the spiritual head of the group, and Frederick Reichert, who became Father Rapp's son by adoption and changed his name to Rapp, was the temporal leader or business manager of the community.

The strength of the leadership was shown in 1807 when Rapp suspended all intercourse between the sexes. The men agreed to live with their wives as sisters. Marriage was forbidden. This prevented the society from becoming too numerous and enabled the women to work unhampered by children. Converts were depended upon to maintain the numerical strength of the society.

The colony prospered. The first year the Harmonists built their town, which consisted of a church, a huge barn, a grist mill, a number of shops, and fifty log dwellings. At the close of the second year they had under cultivation over six hundred acres of land, yielding a substantial surplus of grain which was sold. George Rapp, who had worked as a vinedresser in Germany, understood grape cultivation, and several acres of vineyards were laid out. The colonists raised sheep and erected a cloth factory that paid well. It was Frederick Rapp's idea that the community should not be purely agricultural but should foster a diversity of industries, and his plan succeeded admirably.

At the same time, he perceived that if the community was to progress along these lines, which were a departure from the original plan, it would have to have better facilities for getting its products to market. Everything had to be hauled in and out of Harmony over miserable roads that at times were impassable. So the society began to cast about for a new site on navigable water. George Rapp, who had chosen the first site, picked the second one, a tract of twenty-five thousand acres on the banks of the Wabash in Indiana. This was in 1814. An advance guard of one hundred Harmonists under George Rapp went ahead to prepare the way for the main body of colonists, who followed a year later. Meanwhile, Frederick Rapp stayed in Harmony to close out the society's interests there and superintend the exodus of the six hundred remaining colonists. The property at Harmony was sold for $100,000, and the transfer made to New Harmony.

Traces of the Rappite occupation are still discernible in the old town of Harmony today—a walled graveyard without mounds or markers where over a hundred of the original settlers sleep, and a number of simple houses built of brick made by the colonists themselves. Overlooking the village is the spot where tradition says Father Rapp often sat and meditated during the decade the Harmony Society owned the town.

At New Harmony the members pioneered all over again, building a new town, erecting shops, factories, and mills, a brewhouse and a distillery, a church, and other buildings. They were even more successful in the new location than they had been at the old. But after a ten years' sojourn here Rapp sold out again, this time for $182,000 to Robert Owen, the Scotch social reformer, whose socialistic experiment at New Harmony collapsed soon after he took possession in 1825.

Meanwhile, Rapp and his German coreligionists had returned to Pennsylvania, where a new settlement was established in Beaver County, on the right bank of the Ohio River, eighteen miles north of Pittsburgh. The new town was called Economy. It was laid out in gridiron fashion with broad rectangular streets, two of them parallel with the river and four crossing them. Here the society continued to prosper as it had before, though a serious threat to its existence developed in 1831, with the arrival in town of a bogus German nobleman—Bernhart Mueller, alias Count Maximilian de Leon—who had come over with forty followers from Germany to join the Harmony Society. The matter had been arranged by correspondence with Rapp, who had consented to receive the new recruits.

The count made a grand entry into Economy. He sent ahead word of his arrival, and the local band was posted on the deck of the church tower to play him into town. He drove from Pittsburgh in a four-horse coach with liveried outriders. He was himself dressed in full uniform with gold epaulets and a sword, an outfit which stood out in strong contrast to the simple garb of the Harmonites, who adhered to the plain attire of the German peasantry. De Leon was welcomed at the church by Father Rapp, after which he went to the quarters that had been assigned to him and his family.

The count lost no time in attempting to get control of the Harmony Society. He pretended to be the recipient of special favors from heaven, declaring that he had been inspired and sent on a special mission to regenerate the Germans at Economy. He made large professions and still larger promises. Taking advantage of the restraint upon intercourse between the sexes, and certain jealousies that existed over the influence of the Rapp family, the slithy tove produced a lamentable schism in the ranks of the Harmonites. The count's followers from Germany did not care for the hard work and the dull life at Economy and cheerfully aided and abetted him in fostering a spirit of discontent and rebellion. When the count had won over a large section to his side, he brazenly proclaimed himself head of the society in a paper signed by two hundred and fifty members. Rapp rallied twice as many in opposition, but the bitter controversy that raged bred a lot of ill feeling, and it was finally decided to compromise with the count for the good of the society.

Accordingly, in March, 1832, it was agreed that in consideration of the Harmony Society paying the seceders $105,000 (less $1,800 which the count and

his family owed the society) the count and those
who had come with him would clear out within six
weeks and his new followers within three months.
Many of the two hundred and fifty seceders were
young people. With the money they received as their
share of the communal property, they set out to
build a new community of their own at what is now
Monaca, ten miles down the river. The new place
was organized along the same general lines as that
of the Harmony Society, but with modifications introduced by the count, including the lifting of the
ban on marriage.

The count was no leader, and within a year the
new society found itself in financial low water. Although the agreement made with the Harmony Society stipulated that the money paid was in full for
all demands, De Leon tried to collect more money.
Defeated in this, he incited his followers to send a
formidable delegation to Economy to compel further
payment. Eighty of the seceders went, but were denied the hearing they demanded at the Great House.
Withdrawing to the tavern for a council of war, they
proceeded to imbibe rye whisky made at the Harmony distillery, and presently again marched to the
Great House, which they threatened to burn down
if refused an audience. The local company of militia
ran them out of town.

The count, with a few adherents, fled down the

river to Louisiana, where he tried a similar scheme, as did his wife following his death a short time afterward. The adventurous count's difficulty as a professional organizer of Utopias seems to have been that he simply could not keep his fingers out of the petty cash, a weakness which was sooner or later discovered. Some of his victims returned to Economy and rejoined the society. The celibacy rule still prevailed, and those who had been married during the secession were again separated.

The following year, 1834, the Harmony Society suffered perhaps an even more serious loss in the death of Frederick Rapp, whose administrative gifts and sound business judgment were largely responsible for the prosperity of the community. But by following his plan the society continued to flourish, and good fortune attended its affairs even after the death of George Rapp in 1847. The trustees invested the communal funds in lands, factories, mines, oil wells, railroads, a bank, and other enterprises. The society was reputed to be fabulously rich. Actually, at one time it was very wealthy.

Eventually, however, its resources and membership dwindled. Its closing years were clouded with endless lawsuits, but it was kept going as long as there were any members dependent on it. In 1905, exactly one hundred years after the organization of the society, its only two surviving members began the task of winding up its affairs. The following year the Harmony Society ceased to exist.

Meanwhile, in 1901, the American Bridge Company had purchased a large section of the society's Economy land on which it erected a vast structural steel works. So important did this industry prove to the town that Economy was finally rechristened Ambridge after the bridge company. Yet in the heart of the modern steel city a score or more of the old brick buildings of the Harmony Society still stand, including the church designed by Frederick Rapp, with its tower platform where the band played in welcome to Count de Leon and where Father Rapp used to expound the simple religious doctrines that inspired him and his remarkable community.

Of the galaxy of men who founded Edens, Erewhons, and Shangri-las in Pennsylvania, the most colorful leader was the "madcap fiddler," Ole Bull, who, in 1852, purchased an extensive tract of heavily timbered land in the rugged, mountainous country of northern Pennsylvania, where he planned to establish a Utopia for poor and oppressed peasants from his native Norway. As a renowned violin virtuoso, Bull had made money from his concert tours and was the solitary backer of his colonial dream of a New Norway under the American flag.

Born in Bergen in 1810, Ole Bull came to this country for his first concert tour in 1843, when he was already an almost legendary figure. The most wildly romantic tales were told of this tall, blond, Viking violinist, whose brilliant playing enchanted all classes of people. His tour was phenomenally successful. The excitement his visit caused was surpassed only by that created later by Jenny Lind; and the violinist did not have P. T. Barnum to exploit him. But Ole Bull, sparkling with diamonds, was a pretty good showman in his own right.

It was at the time of his second visit to America in 1852 that he became imbued with the idea of helping his fellow countrymen by establishing for them a democratic haven in this country where they could dwell in peace. Norway was then under the king of Sweden, and Ole Bull was a zealous patriot. Following the close of his concert tour in June, he began looking for a suitable site. At first he thought of locating his colony in Virginia, but in Philadelphia he met John F. Cowan of Williamsport, Pennsylvania, and a member of the Philadelphia bar named Joseph T. Bailey. These two persuaded Bull that Cowan possessed the perfect spot for his colony—a tract of land bordering Kettle Creek in the southern part of Potter County at the headwaters of the West Branch of the Susquehanna River. As a result of this meeting, the violinist took a hasty look at the wild stretch of backwoods country and bought it. It was madness to purchase such steep, rocky, and densely wooded land for agricultural purposes, as it was good only for goats, but Ole was anxious to get his colony going, and the region reminded him of Norway.

Bull was made president of the company that was formed to carry out his project. Cowan was chosen superintendent and general manager and Bailey elected treasurer. Bull put up $25,000 to finance the organization. It was planned to have the tract surveyed and laid out in small farms which were to be disposed of to the fiddler's fellow countrymen at prices that would cover the cost and on such easy terms of payment that each colonist could become an independent landowner. Each town was to have a church, and each district a schoolhouse where the children could learn the English language.

In New York, Ole Bull got together a scratch crew of thirty Scandinavian carpenters, joiners, masons, and other artisans, whom he told to meet him near the point where he purposed to commence his colony. The ceremony attending the settlement of the land took place in September.

"Early on the morning of the eighth," says a contemporary account, "the carpenters commenced working on the new hotel; lots were selected on which to build a blacksmith's shop, barn, storehouse, etc., and Ole Bull was busy with his engineer, taking a cursory survey of the country for several miles around the settlement. About ten o'clock, wagons loaded with stores, provisions, etc., arrived from Coudersport, which Mr. Bull had engaged to follow the emigrants; also a yoke of working oxen, and a fine fat ox for beef, which was soon slaughtered and taken care of. After dinner, Ole Bull selected a site for a house for himself, and also sites for some twenty-five other houses, which are to be put up immediately, to accommodate his Norwegian emigrants as fast as they arrive. Following the creek down about a mile we found an island containing about twenty-five acres of excellent land. This Mr. Bull instantly selected for his garden; where nurseries for every kind of fruit trees, suitable to the climate, will be commenced, and the cultivation of garden vegetables, and the raising of seeds, will be carried on in a skilful and scientific manner.

"While Mr. Bull was engaged in this way, some of us were busy preparing for naming and inaugurating the new place. As a flag staff was needed, a beautiful straight evergreen was cut down, which the Norwegians trimmed, leaving the topmost branches as an ornament to the flag staff. This they raised from the top of the hotel; as soon as it was elevated and fastened, a large flock of birds came and perched upon it, and commenced singing in the gayest and most delightful manner. It appeared as though they were inspired by the scene, and were giving welcome to the great Norwegian and his followers. Regarding it as a good omen, we all united in giving the birds a hearty round of applause.

"It had been arranged that the name by which the town was to be known, should be pronounced as soon as the flag had reached its proper elevation. The cords for raising the flag were now adjusted, and all waited to hear the chosen name. The flag ascended slowly and gracefully to its place, a gentle breeze floated it proudly in mid air, and the name OLEANA was given to the new home of the Norwegians. Thirty-one cheers (one for each state) were given, and three for Ole Bull.

"Mr. Bull then started with his engineer, to select sites for mills. They found an excellent water power; and a saw mill, grist mill, cabinet maker's shop, etc., will be erected in season to meet the wants of the settlers; a suitable place was also reserved for a tannery; proper places for a church and school house were also selected. Everything passed under the eye of Ole Bull; his intuitive quickness of perception, untiring energy, soundness of judgment, promptness of decision, and capacity of physical endurance, are absolutely beyond conception.

"In the evening there was a grand celebration in honor of the founding of the town. Bonfires were lighted in every direction; Ole Bull made a speech to his countrymen, in which, after alluding in eloquent terms to the original discovery of this country

by Norwegians, he counselled them not to disappoint
the confidence of the Americans, 'but by lives of
industry and honesty, to show to their new brothers
that they have not misplaced their friendship.' The
emotion with which this speech was received (of
which the above is but a faint outline) cannot be described; the Norwegians, with bare heads, and hands
raised to heaven, swore they would obey the laws of
the country, and do their utmost to be worthy of
their protection. After silence was restored, Ole Bull
took his violin, and commenced an anthem suitable
to the occasion. No language can describe this music
—the audience, the attendant circumstances, and
the occasion, appeared to have given a new and un-
earthly inspiration to the great artist; he touched
every chord of every heart in his audience. At times
the Norwegians wept like children, as the strains reminded them of kindred and friends far beyond the
ocean, and then the strains of liberty would pour
forth from the enchanted instrument. In a moment,
understanding the language of the music, they
would shout loud huzzas, and chant in unison the
war songs and hymns of liberty of old Norway."

Colonists flocked by the hundreds to Bull's backwoods Utopia. Four towns were laid out—Oleana,
New Bergen, New Norway, and Valhalla. But the
venture was doomed from the start. It cost more
money than Bull had or could get from concertizing

to run the place. It was discovered that instead of having title to 120,000 acres of land, he actually owned only about 10,000 acres. There were stories that Bull had been swindled, though this is doubtful. Anyway, within a year the bubble burst. Cowan bought the land back from Bull, who resigned from the company, and the eight hundred disillusioned colonists dispersed. Oleana, New Bergen, New Norway, and Valhalla became ghost towns. The foundation walls of Ole Bull's castle on the mountain top overlooking the valley are all that remain today to mark this noble experiment. On May Seventeenth, Norway's Independence Day, and on the Fourth of July, the American and Norwegian flags are flown over the ruins.

A curious footnote to this Utopian tale is mentioned by Mortimer Smith in his *Life of Ole Bull*. At the height of the boom Ole bought a gross of plug hats from a New York hatter and had them sent to the store in Oleana, hoping the settlers would adopt them as the official Utopian headgear; but high silk toppers are hardly the thing to wear in the woods, and the stovepipes remained unsold. Henry Petersen, who was Bull's secretary and storekeeper and one of the few colonists who stayed at Oleana, auctioned the hats off to the lumberjacks who moved into the region when it became a center of the lumbering industry. Fifty years afterward it was not unusual of a Saturday night to see men hanging around the store wearing these moth-eaten relics of the Utopian age. But there are no lumberjacks in Oleana today, as the region is now a state forest—Ole Bull Park.

The failure of one Utopia after another seems to have exercised no deterring influence on the visionary zealots with peculiar views bent on establishing earthly paradises. Nor apparently did one profit by the mistakes of the others. Ole Bull, for example, might have learned from the blunder made by Horace Greeley's Sylvania Association in choosing its site in Pike County, Pennsylvania, not to select land of a similar character in Potter County. The hilly Sylvania domain abounded in rocks, rattlesnakes, and other obstacles to farming. Pennsylvania was a popular location for experimental colonies because land was plentiful and cheap and anyone with a Utopian plan in his pocket could get a tract large enough for a dukedom on very reasonable terms; but whether it was suitable for colonization or not was another matter. There is no doubt that some promoters chose the sites they did because they could not afford better ones.

The Sylvania Association was launched in 1843, the same year that Ole Bull first took the country by storm. It was formed by people in New York and Albany, mainly young mechanics or persons in the vigor of life who recognized "labor as the true and noble destiny of man." They founded their colony on the lines of social reform propounded by the French Utopian Charles Fourier. Great benefits were anticipated from the Fourieristic scheme, which provided for communities of about 1,600 persons owning and cultivating their own domain in common and dwelling together in one or more immense mansions called phalansteries, thereby avoiding the expense of separate house building and housekeeping and abolishing the distinction between master and servant. Fourier, who thought of everything, recommended that advantage be taken of the natural liking which children have for dirt to use them as public scavengers.

A young man named Arthur Brisbane, whose book *The Social Destiny of Man* was published in 1840, was responsible for introducing Fourier's teachings into this country. Not only did Horace Greeley become an enthusiastic supporter of Brisbane's plan to establish a Fourieristic Utopia in America, but Brook Farm in Massachusetts, after it had been going for three years, was reorganized as a Fourierist Phalanx. Between 1843 and 1845 no fewer than seven of these communities were started in Pennsylvania. Of these the Sylvania Association was one of the most important.

Any person of good character could become a

member of the association by owning a share ($25) and laboring on the domain under the rules of the association. Labor was to be paid for on a graduated scale, according to whether it was considered more or less repulsive, necessary, useful, or agreeable. Members were at liberty to pursue any branch of employment they selected, but all labor performed had to be for the benefit of the association. All disputes had to be settled by arbitration, with the privilege of appeal to the supreme court of the colony. Any member who sought legal redress outside the colony was expelled. Women were to receive five-eighths of the wages of a man, children from ten to fifteen years of age one-third, from fifteen to eighteen one-half. Profits were to be divided annually, but all balances due individuals above their board, clothing, and other items of expenditure were credited as stock. A library and suitable apartments for public exercises and amusements were to be provided. The association could not suppress any public amusement, nor exclude wine or ardent spirits from the tables of the association, but was bound to furnish them to any person desirous of using them, just as wearing apparel and other articles were supplied. Drunkenness, however, subjected the guilty party to public rebuke, fine, or expulsion. The association could not hire a minister, but was obliged to provide space where one invited and paid by the members could preach. The great edifice to be built wàs to be leased according to an assessment on the various apartments at the annual rate of ten per cent of the cost. Members wishing to eat their meals separately could do so by paying extra, and could use any additional furniture at their own expense. Children under ten and the aged and infirm were at the charge of the association. Young women could vote at the age of eighteen, young men at twenty. If too many selected the same occupation, the supernumeraries were to be detached by lot.

Early in April, about 2,300 acres of land were purchased, and a pioneer division of forty persons entered upon the possession and improvement of it. Less than one hundred acres had been cleared before the association bought the tract. They found upon it a saw mill, an unfurnished grist mill, three dwellings, and a few other farm structures. Other buildings were erected to accommodate new arrivals and to house the various manufacturing enterprises on which the colony proposed to embark. Additional land was cleared and crops were planted, but the yield was disappointing, and the second season was not much better than the first. This was intensely dampening to the spirits, but as an offset the wagons and shoes made by the colonists sold well in the neighborhood, though the market was limited owing to the scarcity of the population. A pair of rattlesnake-skin slippers made by one of the shoe-makers was sent to Horace Greeley.

Despite dissentions and desertions, the colonists struggled bravely to maintain their position, though it was apparent that they were fighting a losing battle. There was something bleakly fine in the way they hung on, but their hopes were finally blasted on July 4, 1845, when an unprecedented and ruinous frost killed everything they had planted. A few days later, when the numbed rattlesnakes were beginning to get around again, there was no one left in Sylvania.

Unique among the many idealistic communities that were founded in Pennsylvania was the Seventh Day German Baptist monastic community at Ephrata on the banks of Cocalico Creek in Lancaster County. It was established early in the eighteenth century by Conrad Beissel, an eccentric mystic, after he had quarreled with the Dunkers, the sect to which he belonged, and had gone off to live by himself in the wilderness.

Ephrata in the olden days was better known among the Pennsylvania Germans by the name of *Kloster* (Cloister) or Dunkerstown, a nickname from Dunker or Tunker, corruptions of *Täufer*, Baptist. The society of Ephrata, however, was a separate sect from the Dunkers. The members, says Julius Friedrich Sachse in *The German Sectarians of Penn-*

sylvania, 1708-1800, "lived according to the esoteric teachings, practised the mystical rites, and sought for both physical and spiritual regeneration according to the secret ritual as taught by the ascetic philosophers of old."

The history of this peculiar celibate sect and its self-sustaining community where the monastic arts flourished was sketched by Dr. William M. Fahnestock in an article in Hazard's *Register of Pennsylvania* for March, 1835. The following extracts are from his now more or less classic account of Ephrata.

"In the year 1708, Alexander Mack, of Schriesheim, and seven others, in Schwardzenam, Germany, met together regularly to examine the New Testament, and to ascertain the obligations it imposes on professing Christians; determining to lay aside all preconceived opinions and traditional observances. Their inquiries resulted in the formation of the society now called Dunkers, or First Day German Baptists. Persecuted as they grew into importance, some were driven into Holland, some to Creyfels, in the Duchy of Cleves, and the mother church voluntarily removed to Serustervin in Friesland; and thence emigrated to America in 1719, and dispersed to different parts—to Germantown, Skippack, Oley, Conestoga, and elsewhere. Soon after a church was established at Muelback (Mill Creek) in this county.

"Of this community was Conrad Beissel, a native of Germany. He had been a Presbyterian, and fled from the persecutions of that period. Intent upon ascertaining the true obligations of the word of God, he conceived that there was an error among the Dunkers, and that the seventh day was commanded to be observed as the sabbath. In 1725 he published a tract on this subject, which created excitement in the society at Mill Creek; and he in consequence retired secretly to a cell near the Cocalico, which had previously been occupied by one Elimelech, a hermit. When his place of retirement, unknown for a long time, was discovered, many of the Mill Creek society, who coincided in his opinions, settled around him in solitary cottages. They adopted the original sabbath—the seventh day—for public worship in the year 1728, which has ever since been observed by them.

"In 1732, the solitary was changed for a conventual life, and a Monastic Society was established as soon as the first buildings erected for that purpose were finished—in May, 1733. The habit of the Capuchins or White Friars was adopted by both the brethren and sisters, which consisted of a shirt, trousers, and vest, with a long white gown and cowl, of woollen in winter, and linen in summer. The sisters wore petticoats instead of trousers, and had some peculiarity in the shape of the cowl.

"Monastic names were given to all who entered the cloister. Onesimus (Israel Eckerlin) was constituted Prior, who was succeeded by Jabez, (Peter Miller); and the title of Father—spiritual father—was bestowed by the society upon Beissel, whose monastic name was Friedsam; to which the brethren afterwards added, Gottrecht—implying, together, Peaceable, God-right. In the year 1740, there were thirty-six single brethren in the cloisters, and thirty-five sisters; and at one time the society, including the members living in the neighborhood, numbered nearly three hundred.

"The first buildings of the society, of any consequence, were Kedar and Zion—a meeting house and convent, which were erected on the hill called Mount Zion. They afterwards built larger accommodations, in the meadow below, comprising a Sisters' House called Sharon, to which is attached a large Chapel, and Saal, for the purpose of holding the Agapas or Love Feasts;—a Brothers' House, called Bethania, with which is connected the large meeting-room, with galleries, in which the whole society assembled for public worship, in the days of their prosperity, and which are still standing, surrounded by smaller buildings, which were occupied as printing-office, bake-house, school-house, almonry, and others for different purposes; on one of which, a one-story house, the town clock is erected.

"The buildings are singular, and of very ancient architecture—all the outside walls being covered with shingles. The two houses for the brethren and sister are very large, being three and four stories high; each has a chapel for their night meetings, and the main buildings are divided into small apartments, (each containing between fifty and sixty,) so that six dormitories, which are barely large enough to contain a cot, (in early days a bench and billet of wood for the head,) a closet, and an hour-glass, surround a common room, in which each sub-division pursued their respective avocations. On entering these silent cells, and traversing the long narrow passages, visitors can scarcely divest themselves of the feeling of walking the tortuous windings of some old castle, and breathing in the hidden recesses of romance. The ceilings have an elevation of but seven feet, the passages leading to the cells, or Kammers, as they are styled, and through the different parts of both convents, are barely wide enough to admit one person, for when meeting a second, one has always to retreat;—the dens of the Kammers are but five feet high, and twenty inches wide, and the window, for each has but one, is only eighteen by twenty-four inches; the largest windows, affording light to the meeting rooms, are but thirty-four inches. The walls of all the rooms, including the meeting room, the chapels, the Saals, and even the Kammers, or dormitories, are hung and nearly covered with large sheets of elegant penmanship, or ink-paintings,—many of which are texts from Scriptures, done in a very handsome manner, in ornamented Gothic letters, called in the German Fractur-schriften."

Several of the original buildings remain at the Ephrata Cloisters, including the Sisters' House or Sharon, the Meeting House or Saal, and the Alms House or Almonry. But the Brothers' House, Bethania, no longer exists. An ancient barn and a number of other structures are scattered about the grounds.

The society owned a grist mill, a paper mill, a printing plant, and a fulling mill. *The Martyr's Mirror*, printed at Ephrata in 1748, was the largest book—it was a quarto of about 1,500 pages—published in the Colonies. All society property was held in common, as was the labor of the members, but individuals were not required to relinquish private property which they held before joining the society.

No monastic vows were taken, nor was there any written covenant. The Bible was their rule of faith, covenant, and code of laws. They observed the original Sabbath (Saturday), and celebrated the Lord's supper at night, washing at the same time each others' feet. They administered trine immersion, with the laying on of hands while the recipient knelt in the water. They did not approve of paying ministers a salary, believing that the gospel was sent without money and without price.

Although opposed to bearing arms, they cheerfully opened their houses to the distressed inhabitants of the frontier during the French and Indian War. After the battle of Brandywine, the whole place was opened to receive the American wounded, who were taken there in wagons. The Sabbath School was converted into a hospital. The camp fever broke out, and one hundred and fifty died. They were buried on top of Mount Zion.

"Celibacy," said Dr. Fahnestock, "they consider a virtue, but never require it, nor do they take any vows in reference to it. They never prohibited marriage, and lawful intercourse between the sexes, as is stated by some writer; but when two concluded to be joined in wedlock, they were aided by the society. Celibacy was urged as being more conducive to a holy life; for Paul saith, 'They that are after the flesh, do mind the things of the flesh; but they that are after the Spirit, the things of the Spirit.' This was a fond, cherished subject, and was constantly inculcated. It may be considered the ground of the Institution at Ephrata, whose prosperity and advancement was dependent on its being properly appreciated. It was sedulously kept before them by their ministers, in its brightest colors. It was a prolific subject for many of their hymns, which seemed to hallow and sanctify virginity.

"It is not one of their customs to wear long beards, as is frequently said of them, this is more the case with the Dunkers and Mennonists. They are often represented as living on vegetables,—the rules of the society forbidding meats, for the purpose of mortifying the natural appetite,—and also as lying on wooden benches, with billets of wood for pillows, as an act of penance. The true reason and explanation of this matter is, that both were done from considerations of economy. Their circumstances were very restricted, and their undertaking great. They studied the strictest simplicity and economy in all their arrangements; wooden flagons, wooden goblets, turned wooden trays, were used in administering the communion; and the same goblets are still in use, though they have been presented with more costly ones. Even the plates off of which they ate were octangular pieces of thin poplar boards,—their forks and candlesticks were of wood,—and also every other article that could be made of that material, was used by the whole community. After they were relieved from the pressure of their expensive enterprise in providing such extensive accommodations, they enjoyed the cot for repose, and many other of the good things of life; though temperance in eating and drinking was scrupulously regarded.

"Conrad Beissel died in July, 1768; and although his successor, Peter Miller, is spoken of as a man of much greater powers of mind, yet the establishment began to decline about the year 1777. The institution was more in accordance with the German manners and notions of the 17th century, than with the new ideas in regard to religion, politics, and social life introduced by the Revolution."

Disbanding Utopias came to be quite as much of a custom in Pennsylvania as establishing them.

PENNSYLVANIA was the first state to pull itself out of the mud. In 1792 it authorized a private company to construct a macadamized road from Philadelphia to Lancaster, a distance of sixty-two miles, and this turnpike, completed in 1794 at a cost of $465,000, was the first hard-surfaced road of any consequence in America. Between that time and the War of 1812 private enterprise added substantially to the mileage of passable roads in the state, and by

1832 Pennsylvania had a network of some three thousand miles of good highways.

Traffic on the Philadelphia-Lancaster pike was heavy from the start. Along it rattled speedy four-horse stages, sometimes half a dozen together, which overtook and passed the long trains of big, red-wheeled, six-horse Conestoga wagons that necessarily traveled at a slower clip. The arched white tops of these heavy freight wagons, often moving in unbroken sequence across the blue-green landscape, marked the rise and fall of the road until it was lost in the distance.

Famed in American annals for the part it played in the development of the country, the Conestoga wagon was purely a Pennsylvania production. It originated among the Dutch farmers of the Conestoga Valley in Lancaster County, where lived the last of the Conestoga Indians. In order to get their produce to market and haul in supplies, these farmers needed large sturdy wagons that could be used on the roughest roads. To meet this transport problem the local carpenters, wheelwrights, and blacksmiths combined to produce the Conestoga wagon, which became the "inland ship" or "frigate" of commerce and, eventually, the "prairie schooner." These nautical nicknames were not so far fetched as may be supposed. For there was something oceanic in the spectacle of vast fleets of these white-tops rolling across the land. Three thousand of them rumbled regularly in and out of Philadelphia, and as many as a thousand were to be seen at one time with their boat-shaped bodies backed up along Market Street, discharging and loading cargo.

The Conestoga wagon first got into the news in the middle of the eighteenth century. When in June, 1755, General Braddock set out on his ill-starred expedition against Fort Duquesne, which the French had built the previous year on the future site of the city of Pittsburgh, his wagon train consisted of one hundred and fifty Conestoga wagons. These had been procured by Benjamin Franklin after Braddock's agents had scoured the back parts of Virginia and Maryland and failed to get the vehicles necessary for the expedition. Braddock had landed in February at Alexandria, Virginia, whence he had marched to Frederick, Maryland, where he halted while wagons were collected. It was here that Franklin, in his official capacity as postmaster general, waited on him, to see about the forwarding of Braddock's dispatches.

"When I was about to depart," Franklin says in his *Autobiography*, "the returns of the waggons to be obtained were brought in, by which it appear'd that they amounted only to twenty-five and not all these were in serviceable condition. The general and all the officers were surpris'd, declar'd the expedition was then at an end, being impossible; and exclaim'd against the ministers for ignorantly landing them in a country destitute of the means of conveying the stores, baggage, etc., not less than one hundred and fifty waggons being necessary."

Franklin remarked it was a pity they had not been landed in Pennsylvania, where almost every farmer had a wagon. The general eagerly laid hold of his words.

"Then you, sir, who are a man of interest there, can probably procure them for us, and I beg you will undertake it."

Franklin asked what terms were to be offered to the owners of the wagons. He was told to put down on paper the terms that appeared to him necessary. This he did, and they were agreed to and a commission and instructions prepared for him immediately. What those terms were appears in the following advertisement which he published as soon as he arrived at Lancaster. As many of the German farmers to whom he appealed were conscientious objectors, Franklin was careful to point out that none would be called upon to fight.

"Advertisement
"Lancaster, April 26, 1755
"Whereas, one hundred and fifty waggons, with four horses to each waggon, and fifteen hundred

saddle or pack horses, are wanted for the service of His Majesty's forces now about to rendezvous at Will's Creek and his excellency General Braddock having been pleased to empower me to contract for the hire of the same I hereby give notice that I shall attend for that purpose at Lancaster from this day to next Wednesday evening, and at York from next Thursday morning till Friday evening, where I shall be ready to agree for waggons and teams or single horses, on the following terms, viz.:

"1. That there shall be paid for each waggon with four good horses and a driver, fifteen shillings per diem; and for each able horse with a pack-saddle, or other saddle and furniture, two shillings per diem; and for each able horse without a saddle, eighteen pence per diem.

"2. That the pay commence from the time of their joining the forces at Will's Creek, which must be on or before the 20th of May ensuing, and that a reasonable allowance be paid over and above for the time necessary for their travelling to Will's Creek and home again after their discharge.

"3. Each waggon and team, and every saddle or pack horse is to be valued by indifferent persons chosen between me and the owner; and in the case of the loss of any waggon, team, or other horse in the service the price according to such valuation is to be allowed and paid.

"4. Seven days' pay is to be advanced and paid in hand by me to the owner of each waggon and team, or horse, at the time of contracting, if required, and the remainder to be paid by General Braddock, or by the paymaster of the army at the time of their discharge, or from time to time, as it shall be demanded.

"5. No drivers of waggons or persons taking care of the hired horses are on any account to be called upon to do the duty of soldiers or be otherwise employed than in conducting or taking care of their carriages or horses.

"6. All oats, Indian corn or other forage that waggons or horses bring to the camp more than is necessary for the subsistence of the horses, is to be taken for use of the army and a reasonable price paid for same.

"Note.—My son, William Franklin, is empowered to enter into like contracts with any person in Cumberland county.

"B. Franklin."

This advertisement was supplemented by the following address to the people, in which Franklin appealed to their sense of patriotism and to their cupidity and clinched it all with the old propagandist trick that is popular even today. He posed the direful alternative. Either they could supply

the horses and wagons at a good rate of compensation, or the soldiers would come and take them
anyway, probably without payment.

*"To the Inhabitants of the Counties of
Lancaster, York, and Cumberland.*

"Friends and Countrymen:

"Being occasionally at the camp at Frederic a
few days since, I found the general and officers extremely exasperated on account of their not being
supplied with horses and carriages which had been
expected from this province, as most able to furnish them; but, through the discussion of our governor and Assembly, money had not been provided
nor any steps taken for that purpose.

"It was proposed to send an armed force immediately into these counties to seize as many of the best
carriages and horses as should be wanted and compel as many persons into the service as would be
necessary to drive and take care of them.

"I apprehended that the progress of British
soldiers through these counties on such an occasion,
especially considering the temper they are in and
their resentment against us, would be attended with
many and great inconveniences to the inhabitants,
and therefore more willingly took the trouble of
trying first what might be done by fair and equit-
able means. The people of these back counties have

lately complained to the Assembly that a sufficient currency was wanting; you have an opportunity of receiving and dividing among you a very considerable sum, for, if the service of this expedition should continue, as it is more than probable it will, for one hundred and twenty days, the hire of these waggons and horses will amount to thirty thousand pounds which will be paid you in silver and gold of the King's money.

"This service will be light and easy, for the army will scarce march above twelve miles per day and the waggons and baggage-horses, as they carry those things that are absolutely necessary to the welfare of the army, must march with the army and no faster; and are, for the army's sake, always placed where they can be secure, whether in a march or in a camp.

"If you are really, as I believe you are, good and loyal subjects to His Majesty, you may now do a most acceptable service and make it easy to yourselves; for three or four of such as cannot separately spare from the business of their plantations a waggon and four horses and a driver, may do it together, one furnishing the waggon, another one or two horses, and another the driver and divide the pay proportionately between you; but if you do not this service to your King and country voluntarily when such good pay and reasonable terms are offered to you, your loyalty will be strongly suspected. The King's business must be done; so many brave troops, come so far for your defense, must not stand idle through your backwardness to do what may be reasonably expected from you; waggons and horses must be had; violent measures will probably be used, and you will be left to seek recompense where you can find it, and your case, perhaps, be little pitied or regarded.

"I have no particular interest in this affair, as, except the satisfaction of endeavoring to do good, I shall have only my labor for my pains. If this method of obtaining the waggons and horses is not likely to succeed I am obliged to send word to the general in fourteen days and I suppose Sir John St. Clair, the hussar, with a body of soldiers, will immediately enter the province for the purpose, which I shall be sorry to hear because I am very sincerely and truly your friend and well-wisher,

"B. Franklin."

The great and sudden effect of this was that in two weeks the one hundred and fifty wagons and hundreds of packhorses were on the march for Braddock's camp. Practically all were lost in the expedition. "The waggoners took each a horse out of his team and scamper'd." In the advertisement payment was promised for any horse or wagon that

should be lost. The owners, alleging that they did
not know General Braddock, insisted on Franklin's
giving his own bond for the performance, which
he accordingly did. As soon as the loss of the wagons
and horses became generally known, all the owners
came down upon Franklin for payment. He was in
a terrible situation which threatened to ruin him,
but at length payment of the claims amounting to
£20,000 was made.

It is difficult to see how a better wagon than the
Conestoga could have been devised for the general
purpose it was intended to serve and did serve from
1750 to 1850. Designed to carry loads of from four
to six tons over bad roads and through steeply-
banked streams, it was of necessity a well-con-
structed vehicle, with great wide-tired wheels
intended to stay up on soft ground. Although these
wagons were not all built exactly alike, all possessed
certain features that set them apart from other
covered wagons and made them easily identifiable.

The white top of the typical Conestoga wagon
dipped in the center and flared out over the ends
like an old-fashioned lady's bonnet. Stretched over
a dozen hickory bows fixed in sockets, the hempen
cover measured twenty-four feet from end to end,
and at the front and rear peaks was eleven feet from
the ground. Lashed down at the sides and drawn
together at the ends, it protected the contents of

the wagon, which was generally loaded to the hoops, from dust and rain.

To prevent the load from shifting against the ends when steep grades were negotiated, the wagon bottom dipped toward the middle in boat fashion. Indeed, a Conestoga wagon without its top rather resembled a dory on wheels. The wagon bed measured sixteen feet in length and was wide enough to accommodate two flour barrels abreast of each other or a single hogshead.

The large rear wheels were five or six feet in diameter, with rims sometimes nearly a foot wide. Amidships on the left-hand side of the wagon was the slant-lidded tool box with ornamental iron hinges. Just above this was the lazy board which pulled out like a shelf from the side and on which the driver could ride, sitting or standing. Across the rear end hung the feed box. This could be detached and placed on the pole for the horses to eat from when they were unhitched. Every wagon carried a water bucket and a tar bucket.

All Conestoga wagons were painted the same colors—red wheels, red side boards, and blue running gear. There was never any deviation from this color scheme.

While the driver of a six-horse Conestoga wagon sometimes found it convenient to ride on the lazy board, particularly when he wanted to operate the brake, he almost always rode the nigh wheel horse. This was the horse next to the wagon pole on the left-hand side, the off horse being on the right. In passing traffic coming from the opposite direction the driver could manage his horses and wagon better by keeping to the right-hand side of the road, and from this practice of the Conestoga wagoners came the universal American custom of keeping to the right.

Quite as remarkable as the wagons were the horses bred to draw them. America has developed only three or four distinctive breeds of horses—the Narragansett pacer, the Morgan, the gaited Kentucky, and the Conestoga. Like the Narragansett pacer of colonial times, the Conestoga horse is now extinct, and its ancestry, like the Morgan's, is unknown. But it was one of the finest draft horses ever bred, solid, chunky, and possessing extraordinary endurance. It stood from sixteen and a half to seventeen and a half hands high and weighed around 1,600 pounds. Most of these horses were black, but as a result of mixed breeding there were bays, dapple grays, and some sorrels. The usual number of horses used was six, but spans of four and eight with sometimes an extra horse in the lead were also employed. According to Henry K. Landis, who is an authority on the Conestoga wagon and the Conestoga horse and everything pertaining to them, the wheel horses, which had to do the backing and turning, were the heaviest pair, while the lightest and most spirited span acted as leaders. With a load of about a ton to a horse, they traveled at the rate of twelve or fourteen miles a day.

The harness was always the best that could be procured—heavy harness for the heavy spans, lighter harness for the lighter pairs. The owners loved to deck their horses with bearskin or deerskin housings and bridles decorated with rosettes and loops of red trimming. Above the hames was a set of open-mouthed bells, generally four in number, suspended in a bow, like Russian saddle chimes. They were made of genuine bell metal and were finely toned. "In the harness and trimmings," reads an old report, "the owners frequently indulged in expenses that approached extravagance." In traveling through villages and pike towns the sound of the Conestoga bells brought people to doorways and windows to admire the horses and wagons as they passed. A wagon with its six horses stretched out to a length of sixty feet.

The wagoners were a rough and ready crew— hard-working, hard-swearing, hard-drinking. But there was a splendid spirit of comradeship among them, and in case of a breakdown or mishap on the road they willingly helped each other when asked to do so. A curious custom among them was that a driver who went to another's rescue was entitled to the other's horse bells, and the only way the latter could replace them was by helping some other driver in misfortune. At the wagon stands on cold winter nights the younger men deferred to the older ones, giving them the best places near the fire in the common room, where they unfurled their bedding and slept on the floor. Each driver carried in his wagon a mattress of shoulder width and his own blankets. On summer nights they sometimes bivouacked under the stars.

The wagoners drank, sang, and danced in the wayside hostelries. Old Monongahela whisky was three cents a glass, two for five, and a meal, twelve and a half cents. They smoked long, rank, pencil-like cigars which were four for a cent and were called stogies, because they were popular with the Conestoga wagoners. The heavy shoes they wore were also called by that name. The professional wagoners were known as "regulars," the casual drivers, the farmers with their own wagons, were "militia."

The extensive travel encouraged by the improvement of roads largely increased the number of stage houses, wagon stands, and drovers' taverns. On the Philadelphia-Lancaster turnpike there was one for every mile of the road. But those intended for the accommodation of the wagoners were discontinued when the Conestoga team was superseded by the railway and the canal. Upon the loss of their occupation, the wagoners sang:

> Oh, it's once I made money by driving my team,
> But now all is hauled on the railroad by steam.
> May the devil catch the man that invented the plan,
> For it ruined us poor wagoners, and every other man.

The Conestoga wagon moved westward and, in less ponderous form and drawn by oxen instead of horses, became the prairie schooner, the wheels of which rolled across the continent to the Pacific, where it reached its journey's end.

TO BUILD MAGNIFICENT BARNS

IT'S an old Pennsylvania Dutch custom to build magnificent barns and paint them red. Often a hundred feet in length, from forty to fifty feet in breadth, and three or four stories high, these barns are an outstanding feature of the fat farmlands of the eastern counties. For two centuries travelers through this rich region have noted these splendid structures and remarked admiringly on their imposing appearance. "It is pretty to behold our back settlements," said Lewis Evans, writing in 1753, "where the barns are as large as palaces, while the owners live in log huts; a sign of thrifty farming."

Prince Maximilian of Wied, who visited Pennsylvania in the eighteen-thirties, said: "The barns are built of stone, very large, and have, in the lower part, the stables, with eight or twelve doors and windows, and over this is the barn, properly so called. At the end of the building there is a passage where the wagons stand under cover; the windows, doors and roof are frequently a reddish brown color."

The contrast presented between the barn and the farmhouse, the former being more impressive than the latter, often led travelers to think that the farmer was more concerned for the comfort of his cattle and horses than for that of his family. But pride in his barn has always been a distinguishing trait of the Pennsylvania German farmer, and, since there is no better farmer anywhere, nor any richer farm, his system of building would seem to be what Lewis Evans said it was—a thrifty sign.

Many years ago a citizen of Philadelphia, writing to a friend in England, outlined the various stages through which a Pennsylvania farm went in its development from wilderness land to a state of high cultivation, with the attendant changes in the farm buildings, from the first crude log affairs to the great stone barns and spacious dwellings of later days. The metamorphosis was accomplished, the letter writer explained, by three successive waves of settlers, each a distinct type.

The first settler to plunge into the woods was often a man who had exhausted his fortune and his credit in the cultivated parts of the state. Spring was his favorite time for migrating, usually the month of April. His first job was to build a rough cabin of logs for himself and his family. This cabin had a roof of split logs and an earthen floor. Light was admitted through the door, or perhaps through a small window covered with greased paper. Adjoining the cabin was a crude shelter for a cow and a couple of scrawny horses. The erection of these structures was followed by the girdling and killing of the trees on a few acres of land next to the cabin. The ground was then ploughed and planted to Indian corn, which without much cultivation yielded forty or fifty bushels an acre the following October, though the family had roasting ears to eat before autumn. Meanwhile, this settler fed his family on the small store of grain he had brought with him and on fish and game. His cow and his horses lived on wild grass or by cropping forest leaves.

The first year or two the pioneer settler endured without complaint great hardships from hunger, cold, and other causes. His chief pleasures were hunting and fishing. He loved spirituous liquors, and ate, drank, and slept in dirt and rags in his cabin. He could have done with a haircut. Living in the neighborhood of Indians, he was apt to acquire a strong tincture of their manners. As the population increased around him, he became restless and dissatisfied. His new neighbors called upon him to fence his cattle which had formerly ranged at large. Game, which had afforded him an easy subsistence, grew scarce. But his chief complaint was the operation of laws. A strong individualist, he could not bear to give up a single natural right, so he abandoned his little settlement and plunged into the woods to break ground again on bare creation. Pioneers of this type sometimes repeated this operation four or five times.

There were, of course, many settlers who remained where they were simply because they lacked the means to move. John Peat, a pioneer in Potter County in 1811, left an excellent brief account of what he and his family went through in establishing a home in the wilds of northern Pennsylvania. His case was typical of many.

"It was very lonesome for several years," he wrote in a communication to a local paper in 1834. "People would move in, and stay a short time, and move away again. It has been but a few years since settlers began to stick. I made some little clearing, and planted some garden seeds, etc., the first spring. We brought a small stock of provisions with us. On the 3rd day of July I started, with my two yoke of oxen, to go to Jersey Shore, to mill, to procure flour. I crossed Pine creek eighty times going to, and eighty times coming from mill, was gone eighteen days, broke two axle-trees to my wagon, upset twice, and one wheel came off in crossing the creek.

"Jersey Shore was the nearest place to procure provisions, and the road was dreadful. The few seeds that I was able to plant the first year, yielded but little produce. We, however, raised some half-grown potatoes, some turnips, and soft corn, with which we made out to live, without suffering, till the next spring, at planting time, when I planted all the seeds that I had left; and when I finished planting, we had nothing to eat but leeks, cow-cabbage, and milk. We lived on leeks and cow-cabbage as long as they kept green—about six weeks. My family consisted of my wife and two children and I was obliged to work, though faint for want of food.

"The first winter, the snow fell very deep. The first winter month, it snowed 25 days out of 30; and during the three winter months it snowed 70 days. I sold one yoke of my oxen in the fall, the other yoke I wintered on browse; but in the spring one ox died, and the other I sold to procure food for my family, and was now destitute of a team, and had nothing but my own hands to depend upon to clear my lands and raise provisions. We wore out all our shoes the first year. We had no way to get more,—no money, nothing to sell, and but little to eat,—and were in dreadful distress for the want of the necessaries of life. I was obliged to work and travel in the woods barefooted. After a while, our clothes were worn out. Our family increased, and the children were nearly naked. I had a broken slate that I brought from Jersey Shore. I sold that to Harry Lyman, and bought two fawn-skins, of which my wife made a petticoat for Mary; and Mary wore the petticoat until she outgrew it; then Rhoda took it, till she outgrew it; then Susan had it, till she outgrew it; then it fell to Abigail, and she wore it out."

The settler of the second wave pitched in where the first left off. He was generally a man of some property, able to make a down payment in cash for his plantation. His first concern was to build a new log house, usually of two stories with two rooms to a floor. The original cabin was used as a kitchen. He next cleared meadow ground, where he planted an orchard of two or three hundred apple trees. Within a year or two he had built a large log barn, the roof of which was thatched with rye straw. Instead of cultivating Indian corn alone, he began to grow wheat and rye, the latter for distilling into

whisky. But this type of settler fumbled his opportunities by failing to extract all the good he might
have from his farm. His house as well as his farm
showed marks of laxity and neglect. His windows
were unglazed, or, if they had glass, the ruins of
broken panes were stuffed with old hats and pillows.
He contracted debts which, if he could not pay,
forced him in the course of a few years to sell his
plantation.

Yet both these classes of settlers possessed virtues.
They were neighborly, hospitable, and helped each
other in building and harvesting and in other ways
without any other pay than the simple pleasures to
be derived from an old-fashioned country frolic.

The third species of settler was commonly a man
of property and good character, sometimes the son
of a wealthy farmer in one of the old counties of
the state. His first task was to convert every possible
spot of ground to meadow land. "His next object
is to build a barn, which he prefers of stone. This
building is, in some instances, one hundred feet in
front, and forty in depth; it is made very compact,
so as to shut out the cold in winter; for our farmers
find that their horses and cattle, when kept warm,
do not require near as much food, as when they are
exposed to the cold. He uses economy, likewise, in
the consumption of his wood. Hence he keeps himself warm in winter, by means of stoves, which save

an immense deal of labour to himself and his horses, in cutting and hawling wood in cold and wet weather. His fences are everywhere repaired, so as to secure his grain from his own and his neighbour's cattle. But further, he increases the number of the articles of his cultivation, and instead of raising corn, wheat, and rye alone, he raises oats, buckwheat, and spelts. Near his house, he allots an acre or two of ground for a garden, in which he raises a large quantity of cabbage and potatoes. His newly cleared fields afford him every year a large increase of turnips. Over the spring which supplies him with water, he builds a milk house; he likewise adds to the number, and improves the quality of his fruit trees; his sons work by his side all the year, and his wife and daughters forsake the dairy and the spinning wheel to share with him in the toils of harvest. The last object of his industry is to build a dwelling-house. This business is sometimes effected in the course of his life, but is oftener bequeathed to his son, or the inheritor of his plantation; and hence we have a common saying among our best farmers, that 'a son should always begin where his father left off'; that is he should begin his improvements, by building a commodious dwelling-house, suited to the improvements and value of the plantation."

The great barns of the Pennsylvania Dutch countryside are called Swiss bank barns, because they are provided with an earthen ramp with stone retaining walls, like the approach to a bridge, which gives access to the second floor and makes it possible to drive hay wagons right into the barn, so that the hay can be pitched directly into the mows. If the barn can be located alongside a hill or swell of ground forming a natural ramp, the same object may be achieved with far less trouble. In any case, the upper entrance is situated on the northerly side, as the barnyard has to be on the other side in order to get the sun.

The Dutch barns are built of stone, brick, or wood. Sometimes only the ends are masonry, the rest wooden construction, but in the case of both stone and brick barns the southern side above the barnyard is always wood. This is because of the overhang or "overshot," as it is called, above the first story, which extends out five or six feet to form a covered way the length of the barn and to provide additional space on the upper level. Most of the stone used in barn building is limestone quarried in the immediate vicinity. Walls three feet in thickness are not uncommon.

A passion for color is an inherited trait of the Pennsylvania Germans, and of all colors red is their favorite, so it is not surprising that they should paint their barns that color. Frances Lichen, in her book

Folk Art of Rural Pennsylvania, says, "The eye of a Pennsylvania German would be starved by the white, black, and green of New England, and the gray and white of the lovely stone houses of the English settlers were as little to their liking." H. M. J. Klein says, "They love red barns, red cows, red apples, red brick houses, and red geraniums." And a reporter on a Philadelphia newspaper, who in the earlier years of the railroads went on a junket through the state, wrote, "Red paint is evidently cheap in the Lebanon Valley, for all the farm buildings and many of the houses are painted in cardinal. They bring their babies into the railroad cars in red calico dresses, trimmed with yellow, so as to make a striking appearance."

The German farmer, in his enthusiasm for color, was not satisfied merely to paint his barn Venetian red. He went further and decorated the vast southern exposure with great circles, sometimes five or six feet in diameter, containing geometric designs painted in the gaudiest possible colors—compass rosettes, sunbursts, six-pointed stars, spirals, and the like. Doors and windows were decorated with painted arches, and blind arches were used to fill blank spaces. Painted scalloped borders were also used along the edge of the overhang, giving the effect of an awning over the stable door. Sometimes the whole wooden front was given a lacy edging.

These decorations are popularly called hex marks and are traditionally supposed to guard the building against lightning and keep witches away from the stock. But the Pennsylvania Germans do not like to have these painted symbols referred to as *hexefuss*. They are purely decorative motifs, they say, an expression of the folk art inherited by them from Middle Europe, where farmhouses have for centuries been similarly decorated. To say that the number of points or lobes within a circle has a special superstitious significance, or that the number of designs placed on a barn has magical meaning, is to repeat an untrue tale fostered by feature writers of Philadelphia newspapers and witch-hunting New Englanders.

Next to the barn the most important farm building was the springhouse, which provided not only protection for the water supply but cold-storage space for milk, butter, and other dairy products. Melons to be eaten on the farm were placed in the spring water to chill. Whenever feasible, the springhouse was built of stone, a two-story structure situated against a hillside to give access to the second floor.

The cider mill was once a prominent feature of all large farms. There was not a farm without its orchard, and most of the apples were turned into cider. Although he was a New Englander, Johnny

Appleseed began his tree planting with seeds taken from the mash of a cider mill near Pittsburgh.

Cider and apples were largely consumed in the making of apple butter, which was and still is universally popular as a spread throughout the state. In the rural districts making apple butter was a social occasion. People gathered to pare and quarter quantities of apples. The cider was boiled in huge copper kettles, holding thirty or forty gallons, into which the apples were placed—about two bushels of apples to twenty-five gallons of cider. Housewives had their own recipes for the mixture, which was spiced with cloves. After hours of boiling, during which the mixture was stirred constantly, it began to thicken, and on reaching the right consistency was removed from the fire and placed in crocks. After standing a few weeks it acquired the proper flavor for eating.

In Pennsylvania, one often sees old lime kilns where farmers used to burn their lime. These kilns were built by men who went about the countryside and were specialists in their construction. It was trade in itself, and those engaged in it were often characters. A kiln was a one-eye, a two-eye, etc., according to the number of openings it had for fueling. Whenever possible it was built into a bank, so the limestone could be more easily poured into the top. It was hard work hauling the stone, and when the burning process started the kiln had to be tended day and night. The men of the family took turns doing this. Enormous quantities of wood were consumed in lime burning.

There is no doubt that the agricultural technique of the Germans was superior to that of any other settlers in Pennsylvania. They were not daunted by the back-breaking labor of clearing the densely wooded land. They knew the soil beneath the primeval forest would prove richer than that of the open places for which the English-speaking settlers plumped. Pastorius, the founder of Germantown, said of his German colleagues who were taking up land that all "have to fall to work and swing the axe most vigorously, for wherever you turn the cry is, *Itur in antiquam sylvan*, nothing but endless forest."

Many of the English settlers placed very little value on their land, because they thought that after a few years' cultivation it was bound to lose its fertility and remain unproductive for a long time. Men would say that such a field would bear so many crops, and another would produce more or less than that and then be worthless. They liked a farm that resembled an amphitheater, with the buildings occupying a low position, so that everything could come down hill to the house.

In many ways the German system of farming differed from the English method, with the honors going to the former. How well the Dutch have done may be seen in that special Pennsylvania space, Lancaster County, where the descendants of the early settlers still follow the old custom of building magnificent barns.

SHORTLY after 1700, an unknown craftsman
working at his bench in a primitive workshop somewhere in eastern Pennsylvania produced an imple-
ment that was to alter the history of America and
the world. This anonymous worker made the first
great American gun—the Kentucky rifle.

The firearms the colonists brought with them
from Europe were fearsome and cumbersome things
that dealt destruction almost equally before and behind. The fire and smoke they delivered understand-

ably awed the Indians and, where several could be used in the defense of a blockhouse, were adequate to hold off the ill-equipped savages. The muskets were effective at short range against plentiful game which had never heard the report of a gun. But the pioneers needed a better weapon. Ranging the border of civilization, warring with the Indians, remote and alone in frontier cabins, they needed a more versatile gun to protect themselves and provide food for their families.

The European rifle was clumsy, inaccurate, and, above all, slow and costly. It consumed astonishing amounts of powder with each charge and threw an ounce of lead, archingly, in the general direction of the target. Reloading was a task better suited to the workshop than the woods. After the powder had been packed behind wads in the barrel, the lead ball was inserted into the muzzle and literally driven down inside it. This feat was accomplished by placing the ball at the mouth of the barrel, starting it into the rifling with a short rod and a mallet, and then forcing it on down with a heavy metal rod. The whole operation required some fifteen minutes of an expert's time, and commonly resulted in deforming the ball and scoring the rifling so badly that the shot was inevitably deflected. In frontier warfare this not infrequently contributed to the untimely passing of the gunner.

To Make "Kentucky" Rifles

In 1700 the frontier was creeping out across Pennsylvania, but to the north and west along the eastern slopes of the mountains the pioneers were halted. New groups of settlers trickled out from the eastern centers toward this borderland, and among them, shortly after the turn of the century, were numbers of Swiss and German gunsmiths lured by the growing demand for their skills in the hinterland. Several are known to have settled at a place called Hickory Town, which was founded in 1718 and by 1730 was known as Lancaster. It was here, or near here, that the first Kentucky rifles were made.

A single innovation made possible the fashioning of this remarkable gun. It was discovered that if a patch of buckskin or linen which had been treated with tallow was placed over the muzzle of the rifle, a smaller ball could easily be pressed home over it with a light hickory ramrod. Instead of driving the lead into the rifling, the soft patch was pressed against the walls of the barrel, effectively sealing in the gas released at the explosion and allowing the unscarred pellet to be expelled with both greater velocity and greater accuracy. The patches, which were ordinarily about the size of a silver dollar, were usually prepared beforehand and strung together on a string. Occasionally a larger swatch was spread over the muzzle of the gun, the bullet pressed down on it into the barrel, and the patch cut off just above

[95]

it with a knife. In either case reloading could be accomplished in a matter of twenty or thirty seconds, and there were later those who prided themselves on being able to fire four and five shots a minute.

The use of the patch made possible the development of the frontier rifle, and by 1750 thousands of the "Kentuckies" were in use. They were long, light, rugged, and accurate. Instead of the .60 or .70 caliber of the European guns, they were rarely more than .45 caliber. From each pound of lead the frontiersman carried into the mountains he poured forty-five to fifty bullets instead of fifteen to twenty, and there was a corresponding saving in powder. Instead of the revealing flash and thunderous roar typical of the short European rifle, the long barrel of the Kentucky consumed the slow, black powder in its length and smothered the report. Instead of the wobbling, wavering ball of its predecessors, the Kentucky delivered a true, high-speed shot which was fatally accurate up to two hundred yards, a far greater range than anything achieved before that time. Indeed, to this day the accuracy of the Kentucky rifle at ranges up to sixty or seventy-five yards is almost unsurpassed, and the craftsmanship of the men who forged and rifled these guns by hand remains one of the extraordinary accomplishments of the time.

The Kentucky was a lean, mean gun that stood well up to a man's shoulder, fifty-seven or fifty-eight inches high on the average, though some were larger. They weren't made to a standard pattern, these rifles. When a man came into the shop, he told the gunsmith what he wanted—a rifle like Pap's or a long 'un like the Shutz boys had, or one just a mite heavier than old Tillie here. And the gunsmith worked to his order. He heated the malleable iron bar from the charcoal furnace in his forge and he hand-welded the barrel inch by inch around an iron dowel. He drilled the bore with bit and hand brace, trued the inner walls with a silk string through the barrel, ground the true octagonal outside with a grindstone, drove the rifling with a wooden die as a pattern. The stock he carved from a block of cured curly maple in the corner of his shop, and he set the hinged, ornamented brass patchbox cover in the right side and the eight-pointed star of Bethlehem in the cheek piece. With soot and oil he rubbed the stock until he had a satin finish and the grain came through in a deep rich glow. After working for a week at the job, the gunsmith rammed home the first load and flicked a two-inch block off a stump a hundred yards away. It was a good gun, light and long in the barrel. It fitted a man's hand and rode easily on his shoulder. And it had the bite of a rattlesnake.

That this splendid gun, which was invented in Lancaster County and for many years manufactured almost exclusively in eastern Pennsylvania, should have been called the "Kentucky" rifle is a slight but galling historical irony. It was pre-eminently the frontiersman's gun, and at that time the generic name for the frontier was Kentucky. All of the territory that is now Kentucky and Tennessee and beyond, indeed almost all of the land beyond the Alleghenies, was in common parlance lumped together under that single name. Until this new and serviceable gun was produced, the frontier had piled up against the mountains, but with it the pioneers began to break through the passes. Daniel Boone and others forced the Cumberland Gap and, before the Revolution, waves of settlers were breaking over into the rich, unexplored valleys of the Midwest. The Pennsylvania-made Kentucky rifle was the gun that opened the way to the new settlements.

Americans today are known as the greatest users of firearms of any people in the world, and it was the facility they developed with the Kentucky rifle that, more than anything else, first earned them that reputation. The pioneer lived by and with his rifle; with it he protected himself and his family; with it he provided much of the food that he consumed; with it he forged on through the wilderness and out across the prairies. It was his friend and companion. He was fond of it, and the pet names bestowed on rifles are sprinkled through all the frontier tales—

the Bitseys and Betsys and Samanthies and Betty
Lous. When groups got together for any occasion,
skill with the rifle was their first sport, and, when
there was no occasion to come together, one was
made.

Wild life throughout America, especially along
the frontier and beyond, was incredibly plentiful.
In Pennsylvania there were herds of buffalo and
deer and elk. During migration, wild pigeons came
over in flocks that darkened the sky. Wild turkeys
often scaled thirty pounds and occasionally forty.
Small game swarmed on every hillside. From this
abundance the pioneer drew much of his sustenance
—his meat, his fat, and a good part of his clothing.
Nor did he use it sparingly as the Indian had; he took
only the best, and the best part of that.

When the settlements sprang up along the valleys,
and newly cleared fields crept back from the bottom
lands, the farmers began to hate the foraging animals that cut off the tender plants in the row, carried off to their nests the ripening corn, and nibbled
their way across the garden patches. Game could always be hunted in the hills, but a field of corn stolen
meant short rations in the barns and cabins. The
farmers began to shoot marauding animals on sight
and, when this proved ineffective, organized great
drives in which every living thing in an encircled
area was slaughtered. A cleared space was chosen

as the center, and those participating ranged themselves in the largest possible ring about it. At a prearranged signal they started toward the center, shouting, firing guns, ringing bells, beating the brush to drive out any hidden beast. As the circle closed they fell upon the swarm of trapped and frenzied animals and exterminated them.

Captain John Dillin in his thorough and scholarly book, *The Kentucky Rifle*, describes one of the most famous of these drives. Organized near Pomfret Castle in 1760, it resulted in the slaughter of 198 deer, 114 mountain cats, 190 wolves, 111 buffalo, 41 panthers, 112 foxes, 17 black bears, and countless small animals. When buffalo tongues and choice hides and pelts had been taken, the rest was "piled high as the trees" and fired with pine knots. It is reported that the stench forced settlers out of their cabins in the fort three miles away. These drives were frequent and deadly and, though they had their utilitarian aspect, must be classed as sport—one of the first on the inland frontier.

The shooting matches which flourished for years in the border regions were less bloody and much more illustrative of the uncanny accuracy of the Kentucky rifle. Many of them drew expert marksmen from miles around. Not infrequently the prizes were substantial, ranging from a first prize of a horse or an ox to guns, powder, fancy knives, and hunting shirts, and all sorts of minor trinkets. The marksmen shot at several distances, from sixty to two hundred yards, and from several positions, but one hundred yards with a muzzle rest seems to have been most common. The usual targets were split pine blocks six inches square which had been charred and scored with intersecting lines, either vertical and horizontal or diagonal. The modern bull's-eye target with its concentric circles was unheard of, and to this day many a backwoods marksman will refuse to fire at one. The blocks were sold at a shilling or two apiece, and each man was limited to one, two, or three, with the prize going to the best single shot.

Another method, called the string match, was frequently used in contests between experts. A series of boards marked with the usual intersecting lines was set up at the specified distance and each contestant fired an agreed number of shots at his board. Wooden pegs were then driven into the bullet holes and a string passed around them. The winner, of course, was the man with the shortest string.

The "turkey shoot" was still another popular match method. A live turkey was tethered to a stake, usually at a distance of two hundred yards from the line, and the contestants shot at it as it moved about. If the distance was shortened to one hundred yards, the body of the bird was concealed and the marksmen fired at the exposed head and neck—certainly one of the most erratic and exasperating targets imaginable.

These matches were neighborhood affairs, and records were seldom and loosely kept. However, enough remains to demonstrate beyond doubt that the level of skill of the backwoodsman was such that it has seldom if ever been equaled with any gun.

At any settlement shooting match rows of tacks were driven from fifty yards. Not one but sometimes dozens of turkeys lost their heads at one hundred yards. A series of five bullets were frequently placed within an inch of center at one hundred fifty yards. And this was done with a flintlock made without power machinery, with irregular, hand-poured bullets, with slow, undependable powder. These records are the handsomest tribute ever paid to the Kentucky rifle of Pennsylvania.

In the early days of Cumberland County there was a famous crack shot with a Kentucky rifle named Captain Jack, who was also variously known as the Black Hunter, the Black Rifle, the Wild Hunter of the Juniata, and the Black Hunter of the Forest. He was a white man who had entered the woods, built himself a cabin, cleared a little land, and amused himself with the pleasure of hunting and fishing. He was happy and carefree, until one evening he returned home from a day's sport to find his wife and children murdered by the Indians. From that moment he forsook the ways of civilized man, lived in caves, and devoted himself to protecting the settlers along the frontier. A family near Juniata was awakened one dark night by the report of a rifle. Jumping up they saw by the glimmering light of their chimney an Indian fall fatally hurt. The open door of their hut disclosed the Wild Hunter.

"I saved your lives," he cried, and then turned and was lost in the darkness.

He was like a character out of a James Fenimore Cooper novel. It was said that he never shot without good cause, but when he did his aim was deadly. For the protection of the settlers he organized an association of frontiersmen who stood ready to act instantly when the signal was given. Their exploits along the Conococheague and Juniata in 1756 were the talk of the frontier. Captain Jack was also known as the Half Indian. "The company under the command of the Half Indian," said Colonel Armstrong in a letter to the governor, "having left the Great Cove, the Indians took advantage and murdered many." Through Colonel Groghan the Black Hunter offered his services to General Braddock. "He will march with his hunters," said the colonel. "They are dressed in hunting shirts, mocassins, etc., are well armed, and are equally regardless of heat or cold. They require no shelter for the night—they ask no pay." The real name of this mysterious person has never been discovered.

In the history of the Revolution, the Kentucky rifle has left its most lasting mark, for to the frontier marksman and their rifles must go a major share of the credit for the victories which established the independence of the colonies.

Stuart D. Ludlum, in his excellent book *Great Shooting Stories*, phrases it briefly and well when he says, "The combination of circumstances which put good gunsmiths on the frontier where they were needed was opportune historically, because the American Revolution might very well have been recorded in English history as the uprising of the Colonists if it had not been for the Kentucky rifle and the amazing marksmanship the early settlers had developed with it."

When the Continental Congress levied its first troops for the war against Britain, ten companies of riflemen were called—six from Pennsylvania, two from Maryland, two from Virginia. These were the frontiersmen, the scouts and hunters and pioneers who had lived with their Kentuckies always within reach. In coonskin caps and buckskin shirts they assembled along the border, drilled for a few days, and swung off toward the East. Group after group, a few hundred here and a thousand there, turned up along the coast after having covered up to five and six hundred miles in twenty-odd days. Their tireless appearance and their boisterous confidence brought new determination to the hard-pressed colonists along the seaboard and in New England.

The amazement in the faces of the more settled folk in the East encouraged the mountaineers to show off every trick in their kit. They shot apples off each others' heads, split targets at incredible distances, splintered boards held between a friend's knees at fifty yards. They painted their bodies, built bonfires in the village squares, and whooped about them in Indian war dances. They swore sulphurous oaths and moved on up to the siege lines. There, with their untrained individualism and their Kentucky rifles, they staved off disaster until at length they suddenly and unexpectedly won a war. Picking off a man here and an officer there, fighting on the flanks, retreating, dodging, reaching out beyond the range of the British guns, they held the English to the coastal cities and set the cost of subduing the frontier so high that the price was never paid. In that, its part in the founding of a great new nation, was the ultimate triumph of the Kentucky rifle.

For another fifty years Pennsylvania continued to assert its leadership in the manufacture of this remarkable rifle. In 1815 there were sixty gunsmiths in Lancaster County alone, besides many other centers as far west as Pittsburgh, where others had set up shops. Indeed, it was only the invention of the percussion cap by the Reverend Alexander John Forsyth early in the nineteenth century that marked the end of the flintlock and the handmade gun, the best example of which was the Kentucky rifle of Pennsylvania.

PENNSYLVANIA, despite the fact that it has always been a haven for such nonresistant religious sects as the Quakers, the Mennonites, and the Dunkers, has perhaps been the scene of more armed conflicts than any other American state. From the defeat of Braddock at Fort Duquesne to that of Washington at Brandywine and Lee at Gettysburg, its record is streaked with blood. No colony suffered more than Pennsylvania did from the depredations of the Indians. It is one of the consolations of history that horrors more than a hundred years old usually do not seem so horrible, but there are numerous incidents in the history of Pennsylvania warfare which were so terrible that even at this distance of time one is shocked just reading about them.

In provincial days the nonbelligerency of the Quakers often became a sharp political issue, particularly when the fate of the colony seemed to be on the razor's edge. Writing of this in his *Autobiography*, Benjamin Franklin says, "My being many years in the Assembly, the majority of which were constantly Quakers, gave me frequent opportunities of seeing the embarrassment given them by their principles against war, whenever application was made to them, by order of the Crown, to grant aids for military purposes. They were unwilling to offend the government on the one hand, by a direct refusal and their friends, the body of the Quakers, on the other, by a compliance contrary to their principles; hence a variety of evasions to avoid complying, and modes of disguising the compliance when it became unavoidable. The common mode at last was to grant money *'for the King's use,'* and never to inquire how it came to be applied."

When, however, the demand was not directly from the Crown, that phrase was not so proper and some other had to be invented. "As, when powder was wanting (I think it was for the garrison at Louisburg), and the government of New England solic-ited a grant of some from Pennsylvania, which was much urg'd on the House by Governor Thomas, they could not grant money to buy powder, because that was an ingredient of war; but they voted an aid to New England of three thousand pounds, to be put into the hands of the governor, and appropriated it for the purchase of bread, flour, wheat, or *other grain.*" The governor understood their meaning. "Other grain" was gunpowder, which he accordingly bought, and they never objected to it.

At the same time, when any expense was to be incurred for the defence of the province the proprietaries, with what Franklin describes as "incredible meanness," instructed their deputies to pass no act for levying the necessary taxes, unless their vast estates were expressly exempted.

Yet it is pleasant to report that when Governor John Evans, who came over in 1704, tried to trick the Quakers into abandoning their pacific principles, he failed to budge them. Ordered by Queen Anne to raise a militia in the colony, Evans met with little success. Unable to persuade the Quakers to renounce their principles, he resorted to the low stratagem of a false alarm to trap them into conduct inconsistent with their professions. An enemy fleet was reported coming up the Delaware. The governor and his confidential cronies flew to arms. With drawn sword he paraded at their head through the streets, calling on all persons capable of bearing arms to rally to the defence of the city. The people, in confusion, sought safety in flight rather than in preparation for defence. Most of the Quakers retained their usual composure, only four of them taking up arms. The ruse was seen through and proved a reverberating backfire. It was a stupid and abominable thing to do.

In 1755 the proprietaries instructed their agents in Pennsylvania to encourage and in a manner direct the Germans to settle along the southern boundary of the province in Lancaster and York Counties, while the Scotch-Irish, who were also flocking into the colony, were to be located nearer to Kittatinny Mountain in the region now forming Dauphin and Cumberland Counties. There was more in this policy than the mere separation of the two races, though collisions had occurred between them over elections, bearing arms, the treatment of Indians, and other matters. The Scotch-Irish were bonny fighters and were needed to defend the frontier.

One old settler, James Dixon, better known as Scotch Jemmy, was surprised one day by some Indians in the woods and shot at several times. Turning on them, he leveled his rifle and dared the rascals to come out of the woods and give him fair play.

"Noo come on wi' your wee axe," said Jemmy. With his rifle thus presented he continued to walk backward until out of reach of their fire and succeeded in reaching the local blockhouse.

Not all the Germans who settled in Pennsylvania were averse to bearing arms. The Lutherans were willing to fight whenever necessary. When Benjamin Franklin was at Bethlehem during the Indian troubles of 1756, he was surprised to find that the Moravians, who he had supposed were opposed to war, had built a stockade around their principal buildings and had even placed quantities of small paving stones between the windows for their women to throw down onto the heads of any Indians who should try to force their way into them. The brethren had purchased arms and ammunition from New York and kept regular watch. Franklin, who knew they had obtained an act of Parliament exempting them from military duty in the colonies, mentioned his surprise at their warlike preparations to their bishop, Spangenberg. He replied that conscientious objection to bearing arms was not one of their established principles, but at the time of their obtaining the act it was thought to be a principle with many of their people. On this occasion, however, they found it adopted by but few. "It seems," comments Franklin, "they were either deceiv'd in themselves or deceiv'd in the Parliament, but common sense, aided by present danger, will sometimes be too strong for whimsical opinions."

One of the most singular wars fought in Pennsylvania was a strictly Indian affair called the Grasshopper War, which originated in a quarrel between two children over a grasshopper. One summer day when the women and children of the Shawnee and Delaware tribes were gathering fruit together, a feud arose between them over the title to a large grasshopper caught by one child and claimed by another. A question of boundary and territorial rights was involved, and when the warriors who had been hunting together returned they sided with their respective squaws. A nasty clash followed in which many were killed. The Delawares defeated the Shawnees, who retired westward to the Ohio valley.

The scene of this Insect War seems to have been near the Wyoming Valley, where Connecticut had an enclave over which the Yankee-Pennanite War was fought. Adventurous settlers from Connecticut moved into the valley beginning in 1762, claiming the land under their royal charter, which granted all territory lying in the same latitude with Connecticut not previously settled by other Christian powers, as far west as the Pacific Ocean. The Connecticut charter antedated Penn's charter by twenty years, but in 1768 the proprietary government of Pennsylvania obtained the land from the Indians by the treaty of Fort Stanwix. The valley was laid out in manors, and Pennsylvanians were encouraged to settle there. There had been fighting before between the Connecticut men and the Pennsylvanian claimants, and it now developed into a brisk little civil war. There were sieges, sorties, and surprises, as forts were built and attacked and settlements pillaged and burned. First one side and then the other got control of the valley. In December, 1775, an army of seven hundred Pennsylvanians was defeated by the Connecticut settlers near Nanticoke Falls. This setback left Connecticut in possession, and the Revolution ended the first phase of the Yankee-Pennanite War.

Early in July, 1778, while many of the men were away serving in the Continental Army, Colonel John Butler, with a party of Tory rangers and a large body of Indians, mostly Senecas, descended the Susquehanna and liquidated the Wyoming Valley settlements. A handful of elderly men and boys, with a few soldiers home on furlough, marched out to meet the enemy but were overwhelmed by the superior strength of the invaders. Prisoners were put to death by the Indians. The women and children in the stockade, however, were spared. They were permitted to escape through the Pocono Mountains to Stroudsburg, sixty miles away, and thence to New England. Over four hundred persons were killed in the Wyoming Massacre.

A few years later the Connecticut settlers returned. Meanwhile, the title to these lands had been taken from the Penn family and vested in the state of Pennsylvania. Civil war raged again. The controversy was referred to Congress, which appointed commissioners who met at Trenton in the fall of 1782. After hearing both sides, the commissioners decided "that Connecticut has no right to the lands in controversy—and that the jurisdiction and preemption of all lands within the charter bounds of Pennsylvania, do of right belong to that state." To this the Connecticut settlers answered that while the state of Connecticut might have no right to the land, yet the Susquehanna Company, under the auspices of which they had settled in the Wyoming Valley, did have the right. Trouble broke out again and continued until, at length, in 1799 and 1801, the state provided compensation for the Pennsylvania claimants by a grant of other lands or a cash settlement and confirmed the Connecticut titles on condition that the settlers pay the state a small price of from eighty-six cents to a dollar and twenty cents per acre. Thus ended the Yankee-Pennanite War. Neither side dreamed that the territory over which they fought would prove to be America's great anthracite coal region.

The revolt in the four southwestern counties of Pennsylvania known as the Whisky Insurrection was occasioned by the excise law of March 3, 1791, which Congress passed at the suggestion of Alexander Hamilton, Secretary of the Treasury. The Scotch-Irish pioneers of this transmontane section of Pennsylvania came very honestly and naturally by their love of whisky and their hatred of excisemen. In resisting the excise law they believed they were following the recent example of the American Revolution. Had not the first attempt of the British Parliament, the very cause of the Revolution, been an excise law? Their principal crop was rye, but it could not be profitably transported by pack train across the Allegheny Mountains. A horse could carry only four bushels, but he could take the product of twenty-four bushels in the shape of whisky, which was the most important item these people had to pay for their salt, sugar, and iron. Distilling was begun at an early date and extensively carried on in the region. Old Monongahela whisky was famous. The new law laid a tax of four pence per gallon on all distilled spirits. It proved so unpopular that it was with difficulty anyone could be found to accept the office of inspector.

The first public meeting was held July 27, 1791. It was a peaceful assembly, but in September delegates from the four counties of Fayette, Allegheny,

Westmoreland, and Washington met at Pittsburgh and passed severe resolutions against the law. Robert Johnson, the collector for Allegheny and Washington, was waylaid near Pigeon Creek in the latter county by a party of armed and disguised men who tarred and feathered him, cut off his hair, and took his horse, leaving him in this sorry plight to travel on foot. Three men were proceeded against for this outrage, but the deputy sent to serve the warrants was whipped, tarred and feathered, deprived of his money and horse, and tied blindfolded in the woods where he remained five hours. Others were similarly treated, and later there were house and barn burnings.

A most unfortunate case was that of an unhappy person named Wilson, who was of unsound mind. He thought he was an exciseman and went looking for distillers. He was pursued by a party of men who dragged him from his bed and took him several miles to a blacksmith's shop. Here he was stripped of his clothes, which were burned. They then branded him with a hot iron in several places and after bestowing on him a coat of tar and feathers released him naked and wounded. The poor man considered himself a martyr to the discharge of an important duty.

In May, 1792, Congress modified the law by lessening the duty and providing for easy payments. In

September President Washington issued a proclamation enjoining all persons to submit to the law and desist from all unlawful proceedings. Notice was served that the government was determined to prosecute delinquents, seize unexcised spirits on their way to market, and make no purchases for the army except of such spirits as had paid duty.

Disorders continued, but toward the end of 1793 the law seemed to be making headway, several large distillers complying, and others showing a disposition to follow suit. But early in 1794 a new wave of violence broke out. Distillers who complied with the law had their stills smashed. This was called "mending" stills, and the "tinkers" who did the work became known collectively as Tom the Tinker, a term which came to be used to designate the whole opposition. Notices posted on trees and other conspicuous places were signed Tom the Tinker. Menacing letters bearing this signature were sent to the Pittsburgh *Gazette*, with orders to print them, and the editor did not dare disobey.

"Are you a Tom Tinker's man?"

"Hurrah for Tom the Tinker!"

Under the law only Federal courts had jurisdiction over such cases arising under the act, which meant that accused persons had to go to Philadelphia, a long journey from the western counties in those days. This cause of complaint was removed in

June, 1794, when Congress gave the state courts
concurrent jurisdiction in excise offences. But nothing short of repeal would satisfy the Pennsylvanians.

At length the insurrection was brought to a head.
David Bradford, one of the violent ringleaders of
the rebellion, called on the western militia to assemble at Braddock's Field near Pittsburgh, and seven
thousand armed men gathered there. Bradford
wanted to attack the garrison at Pittsburgh, but
wiser counsel prevailed.

The Federal Government now acted in deadly
earnest. A proclamation ordered the rebels to dis-
perse. A requisition for fifteen thousand militia was
made on the governors of New Jersey, Virginia,
Maryland, and Pennsylvania. Meanwhile, commissioners were sent ahead to offer amnesty to those
who would submit. Their mission was a failure, and
on September 25 another proclamation was issued
by the President, in which he gave notice of the
advance of the troops. President Washington accompanied them part way; Hamilton remained with
them throughout.

Several meetings were now held by the people
declaring submission, but the troops continued to
advance. They arrived at the scene of the disorders
in November, time was given for submission under
the President's proclamation, and all those not sub-

mitting were arrested. Bradford, who was excepted from the amnesty, fled down the Mississippi to Spanish territory. The insurrection was quelled without bloodshed.

Not long after the Whisky Insurrection had been overcome, the political climate of Pennsylvania grew very hot again over another direct tax levied by the Federal Government. This time it was a tax on dwellings, which were classified according to their dimensions, the size and number of their windows, and so forth. The tax was largely misunderstood, particularly by the Germans, and in the latter months of 1798 discord became widespread in the counties of Bucks, Northampton, and Montgomery. The tax assessors met with difficulties in the execution of their duties—when the officers came to make the necessary measurements the women deluged them with hot water, and hence the disturbance became known as the Hot Water War.

The leader of the revolt was John Fries, an auctioneer of Milford Township, who had not only fought for his country in the Revolution but helped to suppress the Whisky Rebellion. Fries and his partisans harried the collectors, chasing them from town to town and threatening to shoot them if they persisted in their work. At Quakertown they seized two assessors and exacted from them the promise that they would not proceed with the valuation. On this occasion Fries was armed with a big horse pistol. When he heard that the United States marshal had arrested a number of persons for offering resistance to the law, Fries headed a rescue party which marched to Bethlehem and demanded the release of the prisoners, who were held in the Sun Tavern. When the marshal refused, Fries, who was carrying a sword and wearing a feather in his cap, harangued his followers, who numbered upward of one hundred armed men.

"Now you observe," he cried, 'that force is necessary, but you must obey my orders. We will not go without taking the prisoners. But take my orders, you must not fire first; you must first be fired upon, and when I am gone you must do as well as you can, as I expect to be the first man that falls."

The situation had now reached a point where the marshal realized that bloodshed was inevitable if he held out against the insurgents any longer. He liberated the prisoners, and amid loud huzzas the rescuers and the rescued left Bethlehem.

Among the prisoners was Jacob Eyerman, a minister recently arrived from Germany, who seems to have exerted almost as much influence as Fries in stirring up opposition. He said that Congress and the government were nothing but a parcel of damned rogues or *Spitzbuben*—highwaymen or thieves.

After his rescue he fled to New York State, but was

apprehended and brought back. Found guilty of conspiracy and on other counts, too, he was sentenced to a year in prison, fined fifty dollars, and required to give security for his good behavior for a year.

One of the assessors who testified against him was asked, "Were the people of the township much opposed to the law?"

"Yes, they were so violent I knew but only one man on the same side as myself."

"Would this have been so if it were not for the parson?"

"I am fully convinced it would not."

"Did Eyerman appear to be a simple sort of man, easily to be led astray or deluded?"

"No, he was not thought so; he was always a very good preacher."

Prisoner: "Did I not pray for the government, president, and vice president?"

"Yes, you did when in the pulpit; but when you were out, you prayed the other way."

Another witness said that the prisoner came to his house, where conversation began about the house tax, whereupon he said he did not care whether they put up with it or not, for he had no house to tax. A person present said, "But you have a great quantity of books to tax." The prisoner answered that if anybody offered to tax his books, he would take down a French, a Latin, a Hebrew, and a Greek book and, if they could not read them, he would slap them about their ears till the books fell to pieces.

It does not appear to what sect Jacob Eyerman belonged, but one gathers that he favored the church militant.

Following the incident at Bethlehem, Governor Mifflin, at the request of the Federal Government, called out the militia in March, 1799. The Secretary of War sent a detachment of United States cavalry to the scene of the trouble. Fries and a number of others were arrested for their part in the insurrection, and order was soon restored in the rebellious counties. Tried twice on charges of treason, Fries was convicted both times and sentenced to be hanged. Several of his followers were condemned to imprisonment. President John Adams, however, soon pardoned them all, and two or three years later, under Jefferson, the house tax was abolished.

The so-called Buckshot War in Pennsylvania in 1838 was the outgrowth of a congressional election. The defeated Democratic candidate claimed Whig frauds in one of the districts as the cause of his defeat. Whereupon the ten Democratic return judges threw out the vote of the district, thus electing their candidate. The seven Whig judges met apart from the Democrats and gave certificates of election to the Whig candidates for Congress and also to the

Whig candidates for the Legislature, although these latter considered themselves fairly defeated.

This proceeding was part of a scheme to elect a Whig senator. The Whig certificates reached the Secretary of State first, and since he was a Whig, he declared his intention of recognizing them until they were found invalid by investigation. The House met December 4 at Harrisburg, which was full of armed partisans of both sides. Two separate organizations of the House took place side by side amid great confusion. Governor Ritner, who was a Whig, declared the city in the hands of a mob and requested the aid of United States troops, first from their commander, then from President Van Buren. These requests were refused.

After a while several Whigs went over to the Democratic House, which had succeeded in retaining possession of the chamber and the records. When the State Senate recognized the House, the other Whigs joined them, with the exception of Thaddeus Stevens, who made no effort to join until May, 1839. The House declared his seat vacant, and he was not admitted until he had been re-elected. The Buckshot War is said to have received its name from the remark of a Whig member that the mob "should feel ball and buckshot before the day is over."

When the seat of justice of Chester County was removed from Old Chester to West Chester, opposition by the people of Old Chester amounted almost to civil war. As the population of the county grew, the people living in the remote northern and western parts were greatly inconvenienced by the long distance they had to travel to the county seat at Chester. Accordingly, they procured the passage of a law in 1784 authorizing the removal of the county seat to a more centralized location. The new law provided that it should be fixed at not more than one mile from the Turk's Head Tavern in the center of the borough of West Chester.

The people of Chester and vicinity were furious, and before the new county building was finished they managed to get an act passed by the Legislature repealing the previous law. Nor did they stop there; they decided to demolish the unfinished building in West Chester by force of arms.

A force of men under arms was assembled, procured a field piece, and under command of Major Harper set out for West Chester. When word of the expedition reached the Turk's Head Tavern crowd, preparations for defence were made. A company of men was collected, arms and ammunition were prepared, and grog and rations were issued freely. The courthouse windows were boarded up on both sides, and the intervening space was filled with stones after loopholes for the musketry had been cut. The upper story was under command of Colonel Isaac

Taylor and Mr. Marshall, the lower floor under Patton and Underwood, with Colonel Hannum acting as commander-in-chief. The Chester boys, after spending the night at the General Greene Tavern, appeared early in the morning and, taking up a position two hundred yards southeast of the Quaker meeting house, planted their cannon and made ready for the attack.

At this juncture more reasonable-minded citizens intervened, and bloodshed was prevented. The liberty of inspecting the courthouse defences was granted the Chester non-removalists on condition that they would not damage them, and they in turn agreed to leave town peaceably. The cannon was turned in another direction and fired in celebration of the treaty. There was a flare-up, however, when one of the Chester men struck down the flag the defenders had raised. Incensed by this act the courthouse garrison seized their arms, and it was only with the greatest difficulty that they were prevented from firing on Major Harper and his men. But the incident passed without any blood being spilled, and good feeling prevailed when the invasionists departed for home. No one was prosecuted. The defenders of the courthouse considered the victory to be theirs and sang satirical songs about it at the Turk's Head.

In 1786 another law was passed moving the

county seat to West Chester, where it stuck, and the courthouse was finished. The old county buildings at Chester were sold, but in 1789 the county was divided and Delaware County created, with Chester as the county seat. The old buildings were repurchased for the use of the new county. The ancient stone Georgian courthouse, with its pent eaves, is still standing in Chester, but the county seat is now Media.

IN Pennsylvania, you can have music wherever you go, except among the Amish people, who, although they are hymn singers, have no use for musical instruments of any kind, such things in their view being too worldly. Radios are also taboo among them. Yet Lancaster County, which for over two centuries has been a stronghold of this peculiar religious sect, was once noted as a center for the manufacture of musical instruments. The town of New Holland in particular was famous for its German instrument makers. Organs, spinets, pianos, and hand organs were made here in the decade following the Revolution. And David Tanneberger (1728-1804), one of the greatest organ builders of eighteenth-century America, came from the Moravian town of Lititz in Lancaster County.

The Quakers, of course, have always worshiped quietly without the aid of music. William Penn, in his work *No Cross, No Crown*, stated the principles which he professed and at the same time combated the follies and wickednesses of the church that had their origin in pride. Splendid church edifices, fashionable dress, and ostentatious show, high living and voluptuous ease, the swell of music, and worldly amusements he denounced as evils that overwhelmed the fountain of revealed knowledge. But this did not prevent him from supplying the Indians with musical instruments when they asked for them. Among the long list of things given to the aborigines in exchange for the territory now included in Chester County were a barrel of beer and one hundred jew's-harps. The redskins were very fond of these little lyre-shaped instruments.

The Indians themselves worshiped with song and dance. In his letter of August, 1683, to the Free Society of Traders, Penn wrote: "Their *worship* consists of two parts, *sacrifice* and *cantico*. Their sacrifice is their first fruits; the first and fattest buck they kill, goeth to the fire; where he is all burnt, with a mournful ditty of him, that performeth the ceremony; but with such a marvelous fervency, and labor of body, that he will even sweat to a foam. The other part is their *cantico,* performed, by round dances, sometimes words, sometimes songs, then shouts; two being in the middle, that begin; and, by singing and drumming on a board, direct the chorus. Their postures, in the dance, are very antick and differing, but all keep measure. This is done with equal earnestness and labor, but great appearance of joy."

The Quaker attitude toward music put a quietus on all public musical performances outside the churches in Philadelphia until the middle of the eighteenth century. About the only bright spot in this bleak period occurred in 1703, when the Hermits of the Wissahickon, a company of German mystics, emerged from their retreat on the banks of the Wissahickon in Germantown to play at the ordination of Justus Falckner at Old Swedes' Church in Philadelphia. This is the first public concert of which there is any record in Pennsylvania. The hermit orchestra was composed of viols, oboes, trumpets, and kettledrums. But, while the Quaker influence was strong enough to blight music for a while in Philadelphia, other religionists elsewhere were making musical history.

At the Ephrata Cloisters in the wilderness near Lancaster, the love of music which came naturally to the German settlers of Pennsylvania manifested itself in an extraordinary way. Conrad Beissel, the founder and head of this monastic group of Seventh-Day German Baptists, an off-shoot from the Dunkers, was a first-rate musician and composer who made the cultivation of sacred music one of the outstanding activities of his self-sustaining community. The Brothers and Sisters at Ephrata led a celibate and ascetic life, but, to make certain that they sang well, Beissel laid down stringent rules of diet which he thought would improve their voices. Opposed to what he termed "unmannerly paunch stuffing," he interdicted certain foods on the ground that they fostered worldly feelings of a subcincture character harmful to singers. He put them, in short, on very short commons.

"Care must be taken of the body, and its requirements reduced to a minimum," he wrote, "so that the voice may become angelic, heavenly, pure and clear, and not rough and harsh through the use of coarse food . . . in place of genuine song, only an unseemly grunting and gasping.

"At the same time it is especially necessary to know what kinds of food will make the spirit teachable, and the voice flexible and clear; as also what kinds make it coarse, dull, lazy and heavy. For it is certain that all meat dishes, by whatever name known, quite discommode us, and bring no small injury to the pilgrim on his way to the silent beyond.

"Then there are those other articles of food which we improperly derive from animals, e.g., *milk*, which causes heaviness and uneasiness; *cheese*, which produces heat and begets desire for other and forbidden things; *butter*, which makes indolent and dull, and satiates to such an extent that one no longer feels the need of singing or praying; *eggs*, which arouse numerous capricious cravings; *honey*, which brings bright eyes and a cheerful spirit, but not a clear voice.

"As regards the other common vegetables, none are more useful than the ordinary *potato*, the *beet*, and other *tubers*. *Beans* are too heavy, satiate too much, and are liable to arouse impure desires. Above all must it be remembered that the spirit of this exalted art, because it is a pure, chaste and virtuous spirit, suffers no unclean, polluted and sinful love for woman, which so inflames and agitates the blood of the young as completely to undo them in mind, heart, voice and soul . . .

"As concerns *drink*, it has long been settled that nothing is better than pure, clear water, just as it comes from the well, or as made into soup to which a little bread is added."

The singing at Ephrata was very different from

ordinary church singing. Beissel's musical compositions, consisting of a folio volume of hymns and another of anthems, were written in four, six, and eight
parts. All the parts save the bass were led and sung
by the females, the men singing the bass, which was
set in two parts, the high and low bass. The latter
was deep, stern, Gregorian, like the tone of an organ,
while the high bass in combination with one of the
female parts was declared to be an excellent imitation of the concert horn. The general effect was that
of subdued instrumental music, of something almost
superhuman, quite possibly not unlike the singing
of the *castrati* at Rome in the eighteenth century.
This impression was doubtless a result of the choir's
singing falsetto. The singers, cowled and garbed in
white, scarcely opened their mouths. This threw
their voices up to the ceiling, whence the singing
seemed to come. It hovered over the heads of the assembly as if it were the music of some celestial choir.

These pious singers at Ephrata—bare ruined
choirs now where once the Dunkers sang—possessed
a thousand pieces of music. A special room in the
Sharon or Sisters' House was used exclusively for
transcribing it. Hundreds of books were duplicated
in this way for use in their music schools. These manuscripts, each containing five or six hundred pieces,
were lovingly copied from book to book by the Sisters with the greatest neatness and accuracy. Up-

ward of four hundred of the compositions were written and collected by Beissel. This music is still extant, but with the decline of Ephrata the peculiar and affecting style of singing practised there became a lost art.

Remarkable as was this nest of singing birds in the Pennsylvania forest, its record for devotion to music has since been surpassed by Bethlehem on the Lehigh River, where music has been a cherished feature of the life of the community ever since the place was founded by religious refugees from Moravia and Bohemia in 1741. Bethlehem's record, indeed, stands unchallenged. No other place in America is so rich in musical traditions, nor has any community so piously preserved its old customs. Music is not the only reason for Bethlehem's existence, but it is music that has made it unique and brought it world renown.

There were some versatile musicians among the first Bethlehem settlers who lost no time in getting together and joining their instrumental forces. An orchestra composed of strings, winds, and brass was organized to play at church services. This orchestra, which in 1748 numbered fourteen players, comprising two first violins, two second violins, two violas, one cello, one double bass, two flutes, two trumpets, and two French horns, performed concert music as well as church music, but the two were kept strictly apart. Even after an organ was installed, the orchestra continued to play for religious services. Benjamin Franklin, who was at Bethlehem in 1756, says in his *Autobiography*, "I was at their church, where I was entertain'd with good music, the organ being accompanied with violins, hautboys, flutes, clarinets, etc."

Bethlehem acquired its first organ in 1751, and was never at a loss for someone to play it. It is a remarkable fact that at one time out of a congregation of five hundred souls it could muster no fewer than six organists, each of whom had to know four hundred church tunes and be able to transpose and play them in any key in which the minister might begin them. Among the organists active about the year 1800 were a watchmaker, a bookbinder, a clerk, a tinsmith, a nurseryman, and a blacksmith.

As evidence of the love of music among the early Moravians, an entry in the *Church Diary* for July 8, 1754, may be cited. "Our musicians of the church choir, performing hymn tunes, accompanied the harvesters as far as the river, on their way to cut rye at the new farm, which was put into cultivation last fall; as the weather was fine, all who could assist repaired to the fields, men, women, and children."

What a pleasant picture this presents of the people being played out to the harvest fields to bring in the sheaves! All labor was for the common good in this idealistic community, where music was considered appropriate for every occasion. Hymns were even sung at the bedsides of dying persons, who often chose the numbers themselves and joined in the singing.

About this time at Bethlehem a musical custom was instituted that set the Moravians apart from all other denominations. When a person died, instead of announcing his death by tolling the church bell, as was commonly done in those days, four trombonists ascended the steeple and broadcast the news by playing dirges. A soprano, alto, tenor, and bass trombone were used, and the three dirges played indicated the age, sex, and worldly position of the deceased. The trombone was adopted for this purpose as being symbolic of the Last Trump. There is no doubt the custom was an impressive one. According to local legend, a band of Indians on the south bank of the Lehigh, who were secretly preparing to attack the settlement, were so awed by the playing of the Moravian musicians in the steeple that they abandoned their plan and went away. The trombone triumphed over the tomahawk in a practical demonstration of the power of music to soothe the savage breast.

When a person died among the Moravians, his body was taken immediately to the corpse house, where it remained for three days. On the third day it was removed for the funeral service at the church. Here solemn music was played, and then the procession, accompanied by the musicians, moved to the cemetery, where the playing continued for some time after the coffin had been placed in the grave. In 1746, the Moravians gave an Indian, Chief Tschoop, a fine funeral, burying him to the strains of band music.

The old Moravian cemetery was used for burials from the founding of the town until the end of the first decade of the present century. At dawn on Easter the trombone choir still plays in the ancient burying ground. Bethlehem has had a sunrise Easter service with a trombone choral since its earliest days. Formerly the musicians awakened the people by playing hymns in the streets, beginning at three in the morning. The services commenced in the church, and at a certain point the congregation rose and went in procession singing hymns to the graveyard, in time to meet the rising sun.

Trombones were used in Bethlehem to greet celebrated persons, including George Washington, and, presumably, also Martha, since this is one place at which we know she did stop. She had been at her husband's winter quarters in New Jersey and was returning to Virginia escorted by twenty American officers and men. The party spent the night in Bethlehem, and that night Martha heard the Moravian musicians play.

Bethlehem seems to have kept in touch from the first with music and musical ideas abroad, adding new instruments as soon as they took their place in European orchestras. Many instruments had to be imported. They were paid for out of church funds and concert benefits. Bethlehem's double bass cost sixty-eight dollars. It was a notable day when the first bassoon arrived. In the course of time Bethlehem developed skilled instrument makers of its own, particularly builders of string instruments. That the town was musically up to date is shown by the fact that in 1795 it had a string quartet for playing Haydn's Quartets.

The Collegium Musicum, which was organized soon after the founding of Bethlehem, gave the first performance in America of Haydn's *Creation*. The Collegium was succeeded in 1820 by the Philharmonic Society, an organization that cultivated vocal as well as instrumental music. Following this came the Bethlehem Choral Union, formed in 1882 by Dr. J. Fred Wolle, organist and choir leader of the Moravian church. In 1900, he organized the Bethlehem Bach Choir, which that same year gave the first complete performance in this country of Bach's *Mass in B Minor* and began the series of Bach Festivals that have made Bethlehem famous. Trombone chorals are played from the tower of Packer Memorial Chapel at Lehigh University during the festival, which is held annually in May.

In April, 1947, the Bethlehem Bach Choir of two hundred and fifty voices performed the *B Minor Mass* in the Cathedral of St. John the Divine in New York before a throng of 9,200 persons. Fifty members of the Philadelphia Orchestra and the organ and chorus were under the direction of Dr. Ifor Jones. The performance was part of the 250th anniversary celebration of Trinity Church, New York, which gave the event "in token of its desire to advance and support the finest music of the Christian Church."

One of the oddest concerts ever given in Pennsylvania was presented in a cave near Port Kennedy in 1846. Several hundred persons crowded into the main chamber of the cavern to listen, but it is safe to say that what they heard was not chamber music, because it was a Fourth of July concert. It is more likely that the band played stirring patriotic pieces, like *Hail Columbia!*, the lyrics for which were written by Joseph Hopkinson, a Philadelphia lawyer, under rather interesting circumstances.

In April, 1798, feeling between the United States and France ran high. The two countries were on the verge of war with each other. A young actor and singer named Fox, who had been appearing at the

Philadelphia Theater, was booked for a benefit, but as the night approached his prospects of success grew dim. Fearing failure, he called on Joseph Hopkinson, a rising young lawyer, who was also known as a gentleman of letters with a penchant for writing verse. Hopkinson was a son of Judge Francis Hopkinson, a signer of the Declaration, who had won fame as the author of the topical ballad of the Revolution, *The Battle of the Kegs*. Fox explained his situation to young Hopkinson.

"Not a single box has been taken," he said, "and I fear a thin house. If you will write me some patriotic verses to the tune of the *President's March*, I feel sure of a full house. Several people about the theater have attempted it, but they have come to the conclusion that it can't be done. I think you may succeed."

The *President's March*, composed by an orchestra leader in honor of George Washington, was a popular tune of the day. Hopkinson consented to try his hand at writing words appropriate to the music in time for Fox's benefit the following night. Withdrawing to his library, he wrote the first verse and the chorus, which his wife sang for him, accompanying herself on the harpsichord. The words and music mated perfectly, and before long the song was finished. That evening it was in Fox's hands.

The following morning the town was placarded

with announcements of the new song to be sung that night. There was a full house, and *Hail, Columbia!* was an instantaneous success. The crowd, in a frenzy of patriotism and delight, called Fox back to repeat it eight times. The ninth time the crowd rose and joined in the chorus. Philadelphia was then the capital of the United States, and the next night President Adams and his wife, with many high government officials, attended. Fox scored again and again and again. *Hail, Columbia!* swept the country. A crowd of five hundred persons paid tribute to the author by serenading him at his home with the new national song.

There was a time when Philadelphians used to talk about the musical glasses. This was when Benjamin Franklin, whose name one does not ordinarily associate with music, invented the harmonica— not the mouth organ, but an improvement of the musical glasses. The glasses revolved and were played by applying a dampened finger to their rims. But one seldom hears them mentioned today, and, since the death of vaudeville, performers on the musical glasses are rarely heard.

Pennsylvania, with many different nationalities within its borders—Welsh, Irish, Scotch, and the rest—is particularly rich in folk balladry and has never lacked ballad singers. H. M. Breckenridge gives us a glimpse of one of these singers in his *Rec-*

ollections. Writing of the days when Pittsburgh was a village and the races an affair of all-engrossing interest, he says, "The whole town daily poured forth to witness the Olympian games, many of all ages and sexes as spectators, and many more, directly or indirectly, interested in a hundred different ways. The plain within the course, and near it, was filled with booths as at a fair—where everything was said, and done, and sold, and eaten or drunk—where every fifteen or twenty minutes there was a rush to some part, to witness a fisticuff—where the dogs barked and bit, and horses trod on men's toes, and booths fell down on people's heads! There was Crowder with his fiddle and his votaries, making the dust fly with a four-handed or rather four-footed reel, and a little further on was Dennis Loughy, the blind poet, like Homer casting his pearls before swine, chanting his masterpiece in a tone part nasal and part guttural—

"Come gentlemen, gentlemen all,
    General Sincleer shall rem'ber'd be,
For he lost thirteen hundred men all
    In the Western Tari-to-ree."

The extravagant and flamboyant Heinrich Wilhelm Stiegel, who won undying fame for the superb quality and beauty of design of the glassware which he manufactured at Manheim, in Lancaster

County, and for the artistic iron stoves which he cast at the Elizabeth Furnace near by, was a great music lover who had his own private orchestra. He had two hilltop castles near his works mounted with cannon for the purpose of firing a salute when he visited the country from Philadelphia. The salute was a signal for his intimate friends in the neighborhood to repair to his castle to enjoy the festivities of the occasion, and for all his workmen in the furnaces and glasshouses to wash their hands and faces, take up their musical instruments, and proceed to the castle to entertain the great man and his guests.

TO HAVE A TAVERN IN THE TOWN

AT LEAST a dozen Pennsylvania villages can trace the origin of their names to old tavern signs. The quaintly named hamlet of Bird-in-Hand in Lancaster County grew up around an eighteenth-century inn with a signboard depicting the maxim, "A bird in the hand is worth two in the bush." A few miles away an ancient log tavern called the Cross Keys gave its name to the settlement in the midst of which it stood, but in 1813 the name was for some reason changed to Intercourse. Another Lancaster community, Blue Ball, likewise derived its name from a pre-Revolutionary tavern.

Other place names originating in tavern signs include Red Lion in York County, and Lionville and White Horse in Chester County. The beast on the signboard at Lionville, like that at Red Lion, was rampant and red. Broad Axe in Montgomery was so called from a sign of the 1790's displaying a broad axe, a square, and a compass. A tavern called Solomon's Temple gave the town of Temple in Berks County its name.

Legend says that the village of Trappe took its name from a tavern, one of the first buildings erected in the place, the entrance to which was approached by a high flight of steps, or *Treppe,* as the Germans say. Since most of the settlers here were Germans, it became known as the Treppe Tavern, or more simply the Treppe, and the village assumed the name with a slight change of spelling. Another version is that customers overdoing the "tanglefoot" dispensed at the Treppe bar were likely to find the steps a trap. Anyway, it was no way to build a public house.

Probably the most famous of all Pennsylvania geographical labels having a signboard origin is the place near Philadelphia called King of Prussia. This was a popular name with German innkeepers who frequently used it in the old days. The picturesque old inn at King of Prussia is still doing business. Its antique signboard, showing Frederick I on horseback, is traditionally ascribed to Gilbert Stuart, who is said to have painted it when he was hard up, strictly upon condition that his name should not be divulged. Whatever may be the truth of the matter, the old stucco inn, with its ancient stables and springhouse, its huge chimneys and fireplaces, and its attractive old-time atmosphere is one of Pennsylvania's best known wayside hostelries.

Another famous artist, Benjamin West, painted the sign of the Bull's Head Tavern which hung in Strawberry Alley, Philadelphia. West, who was born in Springfield, now Swarthmore, in 1734, began to paint when some Indians taught him to prepare the red and yellow colors they used to daub themselves, and he had obtained some indigo from his mother. The tail of his pet cat supplied him with hair for his brushes. The tavern sign, which was one of his early productions, was commissioned after a rampaging bull had charged into Strawberry Alley and poked his head into the sanded parlor of the tavern. This was taken to be a good omen; the name of the tavern was promptly changed to the Bull's Head, and young West, who at one time lived in the alley, was given the job of painting the new sign. After his death in 1820, it was purchased and taken to England. Its colors were said to be still fresh and remarkably preserved, considering all the years it had weathered.

West's activities as a public-house sign painter also included the Ale Bearers in Philadelphia—two porters carrying a cask of ale slung between them—and two tavern boards in Lancaster County, the Hat Tavern at Leacock and the Three Crowns at Salisbury.

Very famous in its day was a tavern sign at Newtown in Bucks County painted by a local sign painter, Edward Hicks, who painted the wonderful "Peaceable Kingdom" series of pictures and is today recognized as one of America's outstanding primitive artists. "My business," he said, "though too trifling and insignificant for a Christian to follow, affords me an honorable and I hope an honest living." What a way to talk about painting! He was a devout Quaker, which accounts for it. Sherman Day saw and talked with him at Newtown several years before his death in 1849, at the age of sixty-nine.

"One of the aged and respectable citizens of this place," said Day, "is Edward Hicks, a distinguished Quaker preacher of the Hicksite persuasion. Both Mr. Hicks's father and grandfather were attached to the British interest during the Revolution. His grandfather made no secret of his attachment to that side, and was proscribed; his fine property was confiscated, and he fled to Nova Scotia, where he was murdered by a highway robber. Edward, however, is a warm Whig, (as regards the Revolution,) and a great admirer of General Washington's character. In addition to his other accomplishments, he adds that of painting. A specimen of his self-acquired skill in the fine arts, as well as of his high-souled patriotism, may be seen on the tavern-sign in the village. It is no ordinary specimen of village art, but is really the spirited production of a skillful artist. On one side is represented the crossing of the Delaware, after Sully's design; but, with true historical accuracy, the general is represented as mounted upon a chestnut-sorrel horse, and not upon a white horse, as is usual in paintings of that scene. It seems that the distinguished white charger, so well known to all, was a great favorite with the commander-in-chief; and being somewhat in years, the general selected for the arduous service of that night a younger and more vigorous animal. On the other side of the sign is the Declaration of Independence, after Trumbull's design. Mr. Hicks relates that General Washington left Newtown the same night that he crossed the Delaware. He also says that the night preceding General Mercer told Mrs. Keith that he had dreamed of being attacked and overpowered by a huge black bear. A few days afterwards he was indeed attacked and killed, at Princeton, by the British or Hessians. Soothsayers may draw their own inferences."

Another tale of this region is told of an elderly Quaker sign painter, probably Hicks, who was hired to paint a sign for a stage proprietor and tavern keeper, an anonymous alcoholic of Bucks County. The device was to be a fine coach-and-four driven by the proprietor himself, who claimed that he had occasionally driven his own stages. The work was admirably done, and the proprietor called in for a preview. The driver's face was an excellent likeness, but he appeared to be lolling to one side as if about to tumble from his box. His whip hung down listlessly; the reins were negligently held. Yet the driver did not appear to be asleep. His ruddy face, indeed, bore a remarkably happy expression.

"But how is this?" cried the proprietor. "That is no way for a driver to sit."

"Doesn't thee get a little so sometimes?" suggested the old Quaker.

The man flew into a terrible rage, but the painter finally calmed him down and agreed that, if he would foreswear his cups, he would obliterate the tipsy driver, paint him as he should be, and hush up the affair. It appeared that the man's intemperance was not generally suspected but was known only to the Quaker and a few other close friends. The reformation of the publican, it is related, was prompt and permanent.

Lancaster was formerly noted for its tavern signs. Soon after the opening of the turnpike to Philadelphia in 1795, when Lancaster was a city of fewer than five thousand, it had one hundred and eighty licensed taverns. A writer who visited Lancaster about 1840 said strangers were particularly struck with the numerous tavern signs that greeted them by the dozens along the principal streets. "They form a sort of outdoor picture gallery, and some are no mean specimens of art. Here may be seen half the kings of Europe—the King of Prussia, of Sweden, and the Prince of Orange; and then there are the warriors—Washington, Lafayette, Jackson, Napoleon, William Tell, and a whole army of others; and of statesmen there are Jefferson, Franklin, and others; and then comes the Red Lion of England, leading a long procession of lions, bears, stags, bulls, horses, eagles, swans, black, white, dun, and red— not to mention the inanimate emblems, the globe, the cross keys, the plough, the wheat sheaf, the compass and square, and the hickory tree. These numerous inns, far too many for the present wants of the city, tell of bygone days, before the railroad and canals were constructed, when the streets and yards were crowded every evening with long trains of

Conestoga wagons, passing over the turnpike, by which nearly all the interior of the state was supplied with merchandise."

Since Philadelphia was a port it naturally had many taverns catering to seafaring men. These places adopted salty names and sported seagoing signboards, with such titles as the Jolly Sailors, the Top Gallant, the Brig and Snow, the Boatswain and Call, the Wounded Tar, the Admiral Warren, and the Dolphin, but, alas, no Mermaid. When William Penn first arrived at Philadelphia there was a waterfront inn already open for business under the nautical name of the Blue Anchor.

When Benjamin Franklin, as a teen-age youth, landed at Philadelphia, he inquired of a Quaker whose countenance he liked where a stranger could get lodging. They were then near the sign of the Three Mariners. "Here," said the Quaker, "is one place that entertains strangers, but it is not a reputable house. If thee will come with me, I'll show thee a better." So he led him to the Crooked Billet in Water Street, where Franklin, while eating his dinner, was asked several sly questions. Decades later Franklin's own house was turned into a tavern. During his lifetime a number of inns were named for him. In 1774 a tavern at the corner of Walnut and Fifth Streets adopted the sign of Franklin, with these patriotic lines:

Come view your patriot father, and your friend,
And toast to freedom, and to slavery's end.

The Crooked Billet did not have a pictorial signboard, but instead hung out a practical emblem in
the form of a crooked billet of wood. This was also
the case with other taverns. Thus the Pewter Platter
used a large pewter platter for a sign.

Many changes were made in tavern signs at the
time of the Revolution. The Golden Lion of Philadelphia, for example, became the Yellow Cat. Another lion suffered the indignity of having a crowing
rooster painted on its back with the word "Liberty"
issuing from the bird's beak, while still other lions
were fettered with chains. At Bristol in Bucks
County there was a tavern called the King George
which had a sign with that monarch's portrait.
When the American army passed through the place
they riddled King George with bullets, and the proprietor was forced to adopt the more popular device
of the Fountain. His new sign was considered a masterpiece of art by his rustic guests. As an aftermath
of the war, sea fights became popular subjects of
signboard picturization, with the British, of course,
always shown taking a beating.

Pennsylvania has had some mighty innkeepers,
fellows of Falstaffian proportions, who were hosts in
themselves. The biggest landlord in Philadelphia

was Michael Dennison, a great hogshead of a man, who kept the George Inn at the Sign of St. George and the Dragon at Arch and Second Streets. Michael made a packet of money and decided to return to the old country. This occasioned the following lines:

> His bulk increased by ale and venison,
> Alas! we soon must lose good Dennison.
> *City of Penn!* the loss deplore,—
> Altho with *pain,* his bulk you bore!—
> Michael, farewell! Heaven speed thy course,
> Saint George take with thee and thy horse;
> But to our hapless city kind,
> The watchful Dragon leave behind.—
> Michael! your wealth and full-spread *frame,*
> Shall publish Pennsylvania's fame.
> Soon as the planks beneath you crack,
> The market shall be hung with black.

Then there was Just Johnson, the giant Moravian brother who, in 1777, became landlord of the famous Sun Inn at Bethlehem, the signboard of which showed the sun in meridian splendor then a little dulled from having been out all night for a dozen years. Just was known far and wide for his powerful build. When stories of his strength reached Christian Grubb, an iron master of Lancaster County, also notorious for his strength and for his prowess as a boxer, the latter made a pilgrimage to the Sun Inn expressly to pick a fight with its mighty landlord. Just Johnson was an affable Goliath, and it was not until Grubb had grossly insulted him that he lost his temper. Suddenly grabbing the master by the seat of his breeches and the collar of his coat he hove him over the iron railing of the porch to the pavement below.

"God bless meiner soul!" cried Just. "I drows you over the bannisters."

Grubb, who was no lightweight but a man of girth and brawn, was satisfied with Just's display of strength and took it in good part. He told the landlord who he was and why he had come to Bethlehem, and together they made merry over the incident.

Villainous innkeepers were not unknown in Pennsylvania in primitive times. One of these kept a tavern on the Blockhouse Road about twelve miles from Blossburg, in Tioga County, in Northern Pennsylvania. His name was Anthony, and he was half French and half Dutch. According to his own story, he had spent most of his life as a soldier during the stormy times of the French Revolution. Anthony used to amuse his guests with stories of his bold-faced villainies, declaring that there was not one of the Ten Commandments he had not broken repeatedly.

It's an Old Pennsylvania Custom

"With the habits of an old soldier," reads a century-old account of him, "he had little disposition to get his living by tilling the ground; and found the military mode of pillage much more to his taste. He raised no oats, but always charged travellers for the use of his troughs, and for sleeping before his fire. Whiskey was the staple commodity at his house, serving both as meat and drink. Many of the early emigrants to the Genesee country drove their young cattle along. There was a wide track of some fearful tornado, not far from Anthony's house, in which he had contrived to cut an open space, with a narrow passage into it; making a kind of unseen pen. To this spot the cattle of his guests were very apt to stray, in the night. In the morning the poor emigrants were hunting, far and near, for their cattle, with Anthony for their guide; but on such occasions he never happened to think of the windfall.

"The unsuspecting guests, after two or three days of fruitless search, would leave, paying roundly for their detention; and instructing the old scoundrel to hunt the cattle, and when found, to write to a certain address, with a promise of reward for his trouble. Anthony never had occasion to write; but it was always remarked that he kept his smoke-house well supplied with what *he* called elk-meat. When or where he caught the elks was never known. Some lone travellers, who stopped at his house, it is strongly suspected, never reached their intended destination."

Sometimes innkeepers were victimized by their guests. A common sight on the highways and by-ways of old Pennsylvania were companies of re-demptioners being herded along by what were called soul drivers. Penniless emigrants who could not get to America in any other way would pay for their passage by binding themselves to three years' service after they got here. It was a stiff price to pay, and the poor redemptioners, when they arrived, were sold by the masters of the emigrant ships in lots of fifty or more to the soul drivers, who herded them through the countryside selling them to farm-ers. It was a shameless traffic which was eventually broken up when large numbers of redemptioners ran away from their drivers. The last soul driver disappeared about the year 1785. He is said to have been tricked by one of his own flock, a young Irish-man, who managed to be the last of the lot to remain unsold. On their travels they lodged one night at an inn. The next morning the young fellow rose early and sold his master to the landlord. Pocketing the money he marched off, but not before telling the purchaser that his new servant, though reason-ably clever, was likely to be insolent and a little given to lying. He had even been presumptuous enough to endeavor to pass himself off as master, and might try it again, but the landlord should pay no attention to what the fellow said.

There was, of course, a great difference between town and country inns in the matter of accommodations in bygone days. Travelers complained grievously about the low standards of cleanliness at rural inns, especially in the matter of bedding, but this was characteristic of inns in general rather than of Pennsylvania in particular; though the old Dutch custom of sleeping without sheets or blankets between two feather beds brought protests from guests who were not accustomed to "sleeping between decks," as it was called.

Dr. Henry Reed Stiles, in his book on bundling, tells of a schoolmaster in Southern Pennsylvania, who, though he usually boarded around, sometimes put up at a tavern run by an honest old Dutchman. Applying for lodging at the tavern one evening, he was told that he could stay overnight and, after visiting with the landlord for awhile, he was lighted to his room. The landlord had put down the candle and left before the schoolmaster discovered that the only bed in the room was occupied. Calling to his host, he informed him that he must have made a mistake as somebody was already in possession of the room. "Oh! dat ish only mine taughter," answered the Dutchman over his shoulder, "she won't hurt nopoty," and he continued on his way.

To Have a Tavern in the Town

Pennsylvania has always been well provided with inns, and those under Dutch management have from the first been well patronized because they have had the reputation for offering the best food and the most comfortable accommodations.

When the ancient custom of holding fairs in county towns was more generally observed than it is today, the taverns in the towns did a rushing trade. The following pleasant little account is of the fair at Lancaster when that city was young and gay.

"Annually in those days a fair was held on the first Thursday and Friday in June. You could hardly see the streets for the tables and booths, covered with merchandise and trinkets of every kind. There were silks, laces, and jewelry, calicoes, gingerbread, and sweetmeats, such as the ladies love; and that was the time they got plenty of them, too, for the young fellows used to hoard up their pocket money for months together to spend at the fair; and no girl felt ashamed to be treated to a fairing, even by a lad she had never seen before. This was the first step towards expressing admiration, and she who got the most fairings was considered as the belle. Then the corners of the streets were taken up with mountebanks, rope dancers, and all the latest amusements. To see these, each young man took the girl who pleased him most; or, if he had a capacious heart, he sometimes took half a dozen.

"Then there were the dances, the crowning pleasure of all. In every tavern was to be heard the sound of the violin."

Pennsylvania was formerly always being visited by inimical Connecticut Yankees, and one of these, a self-styled counterfeiter named William Stewart, who visited the lumbering region of the Susquehanna in 1806, describes the primitive life of that section then, when tavern haunting was apparently a favorite pastime of the populace.

"This region of the country was wild and picturesque, and the people generally were Dutch and Yankees of the most filthy, wild, and vulgar kind that could be conceived. I had just left Connecticut and its enlightened communities, and had dropped down as it were among a race as debased and corrupt as those who have already entered the stygian pool.

"But though this state of society was at first so repulsive, I soon got used to it and became somewhat gratified with their rude, drinking boisterous characters. I resolved to stay a year and try my fortune among them. I was engaged in diverse pursuits. Sometimes I hunted bears, sometimes panthers, wolves, deer, etc., for the woods and mountains were overcharged with game. Sometimes we had frolics of the most noisy sort. We drank whiskey, not in half gills as it is taken now, but in gallons, and barrels. Every family had their whiskey cask, and it was drunk by old and young, as plentifully as if it were cow's milk.

"It can easily be conceived what followed such a course of life. Every evening a gang assembled at the numerous taverns to drink, tell stories, and fight. When they had become half drunk, they were noisy and quarrelsome; gouging out the eyes was one of their barbarous practices, and nearly one-third of the German population had but one eye. I saw one day a horse with one eye, carrying upon his back the husband, wife, and child, each with only one eye.

"This eye gouging they called sport, but I thought it dear. Upon every Sunday, crowds collected at taverns, and the day was spent in drinking, swearing, and fighting."

Pᴇɴɴsʏʟᴠᴀɴɪᴀ is great pie country. The Germans have for generations been pie enthusiasts, eating it morning, noon, and night, as the New Englanders did, but in greater variety. America is today a pie-eating nation largely because of Pennsylvania influence. Usually called "Pennsylvania Dutchmen," these people developed cooking traditions all their own through their skill and love for the unusual. Consequently, Pennsylvania pies, along with several other dishes, have rarely, if ever, been surpassed.

Seven or eight pies baked at the same time in deep earthen pie plates and fresh from the huge Dutch oven would emit such a fragrance as few moderns have ever known. There would be blackberry pies, cherry, rhubarb, raspberry, peach, apple, green currant, plum, gooseberry, grape, strawberry, potato custard, country molasses, mince, or pumpkin, to mention only a few of the array housewives specialized in and for which they are justly famous. These pies would be large and deep. Perhaps earlier than anywhere else in America, deep-dish pies appeared in Pennsylvania. Lard, well rendered and pure, would be mixed with flour milled by real millstones, and hands would be used deftly to make the crust— the only proper method of mixing pastry, as all good cooks know.

In Pennsylvania the first specialized use of dried fruits in pies was started. Raspberries, peaches, huckleberries, apples, plums, cherries, apples, or pears would be put into Dutch ovens and dehydrated, slow-dried. The skin was left whole, and thus the juiciness of the fruit was not lost, but rather it was retained and assimilated. On some future day mouth-watering pies would be made of these dried fruits. Apple or pear Schnitz and Knepp was one of the favorite and best dishes. The end of a ham bone containing a very little meat would be placed in a large kettle with a small quantity of water. Then "Schnitz" would be added—sliced, sweet, dried apples or pears. When the fruit was cooked tender in the ham broth, dumplings were lightly dropped on top of the apples or pears and cooked in the broth, too. The dumpling, of course, was the "Knepp" and was sometimes used with stewed chicken as well.

Not only was pie served for breakfast, but usually several kinds would be offered for a choice. Along with the pie there would be cereal or mush, to be followed by sausage with bacon on the side. Drippings from the bacon would be poured over an accompanying dish of pancakes. This was only the beginning.

Philadelphia scrapple, sometimes called "Ponhaus," was indispensable. This dish which, according to Struthers Burt, dates from the early Swedish and genuine Dutch, was made by boiling hog's head seasoned with sage, salt, and pepper, and mixing it with cornmeal to make a mushy substance. The mixture would then be stored in long pans placed in a cool place until it was wanted—which was often—and slices from the loaf would be fried in deep fat.

A really hearty eater could down all this and still find plenty of room for a few fried potatoes, eggs with ham, home-made bread or biscuit, and, of course, another slice of pie.

Naturally, pies were not the only item on the menu that concerned the Pennsylvanians. Food, the variety, the preparation, and the consumption thereof, was always a matter of such importance to them that the average housewife usually spent about one-half of her time in the kitchen, while the head of the household devoted quite a bit of his to slaughtering and gardening. Possibly this lusty appetite is not a distinctive feature belonging exclusively to the Germans of Pennsylvania, for, after all, people everywhere like to eat a lot. But certainly the ingenuity, the originality, and the perfection of their culinary skill raised Pennsylvanian cooking to an art unsurpassed by that of any other section of the country.

The first gourmets of America were Pennsylvania Dutchmen, and the first dining club in the New World was organized in Philadelphia in 1732, a city which was then a center of good food and has never lost its reputation in this field.

By the time of the Revolution, Pennsylvania had already established itself on this score. Washington recognized this with his admiration for his "good friend" Christopher Ludwig, a Dutchman who was appointed by Congress in May, 1777, to be the Continental Army's head baker. There is even evidence that Washington chose Valley Forge for winter quarters primarily because he could depend on the Dutch to provision the men. The Dutch bake ovens used by the Army can still be seen today.

According to J. George Frederick (*The Pennsylvania Dutch and Their Cookery*), these ovens were developed to suit Dutch tastes and capacity for large quantities of food. It would be hard to say whether they developed the oven because of this, or whether the happy invention of the oven made it possible to cook more, and therefore necessitated more eating to avoid waste—something, incidentally, completely alien to the typical Pennsylvanian. Practically every homestead had one of these ovens, an outdoor stone structure, whitewashed and immaculate. The door was breast high and opened so that the oven could be fired with several armfuls of brushwood, or as much as the seven-foot long and two-foot high oven could hold. When the wood had burned to ashes and been raked out, the oven was ready. Loaves of bread, seven or eight pies, five or six crumb cakes, and a huge array of cookies would be placed inside to bake on the bare hearth. Everything was taken out with a six-foot tool with a broad flat end. Then fruits would often be put in to dehydrate since the thrifty housewife took full advantage of every vestige of heat in the oven.

In order to understand the lavishness of the food

on the Pennsylvanian dining tables, it is necessary to remember, as Mr. Frederick points out, that the state was developed originally on the principle of self-sustaining farms. Any surplus of either raw or cooked foods could be sold in the market street stands or stalls of Lancaster, Reading, Philadelphia, or other cities. Therefore, housewives produced food not only for their families, but also wagon loads of it to sell weekly on gala market days when the family went to town.

That the cities profited by this opportunity to buy fresh vegetables, meats, and other farm products is illustrated by a menu for a dinner of the Historical Society of Pennsylvania, served at the Sun Hotel, Bethlehem, Pennsylvania, on Tuesday, November 8, 1859:

SOUP
Calf's Head.

FISH
Boiled Rock, Sauce Monocasy.

ROAST
Ribs of Beef.   Chickens.   Domestic Ducks.
Goose, Apple Sauce.
Stuffed Turkey, Cranberry Sauce.
Lamb with Jelly.
Ham, Champagne Sauce.

[165]

It's an Old Pennsylvania Custom

HOT RELISHES

Boiled Turkey, Oyster Sauce. Baked Calf's Head.

COLD DISHES

Boned Turkey.   Chicken Salad.   Beef Tongue.
Lobster Salad.   Boiled Ham.

RELISHES

Assorted Pickles.   Worcestershire Sauce.
Cold Slaw.   Cranberry Sauce.   Currant Jelly.
French Mustard.   Apple Sauce.   Celery.   Catsup.

VEGETABLES

Turnips.   Sweet Potatoes.   Tomatoes.
Baked Potatoes.   Hominy.   Egg Plants.
Mashed Potatoes.

GAME

Saddle of Venison.   Canvas Back Ducks.
Red Head Ducks.   Pheasants.   Partridges on Toast.

ORNAMENTAL

Pyramid of Macaroni

PASTRY AND PUDDINGS

Mince Pie.   Moravian Apple Cake.
Bethlehem Streussel.   Apple Pie.
Moravian Sugar Cake.   Pound Cake.
Calf's Foot Jelly.
Forms of Vanilla and Strawberry Ice Cream.

To Enjoy Shoo-fly Pie

Figs.   Almonds.   Raisins.   Grapes.   Apples.
Cheese.   Vanilla Ice Cream.
Strawberry Ice Cream.   Coffee and Tea.

This is typical of the holiday, special occasion, or usual feast offered guests. Thanksgiving, for instance, was always a time for well-filled tables reminiscent of Puritan spreads. Christmas, too, was a fete, and Easter as well.

Dinner with the Pennsylvanians was always an event. There was no nonsense about an "appetizer" for the meal, at least not in the modern sense. Apparently all Pennsylvanians were born hungry and remained in that happy state for the endurance of their lives. Soup was the most popular beginning for the meal.

These soups were often enough to make the whole of a dinner not planned for leisurely enjoyment. They were thick and heavy—Beef, Philadelphia Pepper Pot (for which the state is famous), Brown Potato Chowder, Brown Flour, or the Calf's Head that the one hundred members of the Historical Society enjoyed. All these soups were notably inexpensive and were sometimes called "poverty soups."

What Pennsylvanians did to meat deserves its own chapter. Ribs of beef, chickens, game, lamb, ham, and fresh-water fish were favorites. Roast beef would be cooked slowly and well to bring out all the juices of the cut, home-cured ham would be heavy with gravy and covered with pungent spices, a huge piece of pork would be cooked until it was as tender as a young hen, and of course smoked sausage, or broiled or stewed chicken covered with a thick white gravy filled with choice parts could never be forgotten by anyone who ever ate an old-fashioned Pennsylvania dinner. Not only did the average family cook and eat these delicious meats, but usually the slaughtering and dressing were done by the men of the family while the women did the rest of the work.

Accompanying these meats would be some of the most unusual and most typically Pennsylvanian dishes in existence. Vegetables, in the era when traditional foods were being developed, could not be had out of season, nor in tin cans, so housewives had to make the most of the few available by being as clever and original in using them. Cabbage was a favorite that was used in many ways—to make sauerkraut for one. Jerusalem artichokes, Mennonite pod peas cooked in their shells with pepper, salt, and butter, and fried cucumbers were frequent accompaniments to a meal. The Pennsylvanians fried a great many foods. Fried peppers were popular, as were fried tomatoes, fried cornmeal mush, and fried oysters. (Most Pennsylvanians were denied salt-water fish in earlier times because of transportation difficulties, but oysters were popular, as were lake trout, baked pike, shad, and a unique dish called fish macaroni.)

Fried pies, too, were a particularly delicious and characteristic food. Then there were fried noodles, corn fry, and tomato cakes, among others.

Few salads, in the modern sense, were eaten by Pennsylvanians. However, there were unusual combinations the Dutch developed to accompany their richest meals. Hot potato salad was a particular delicacy developed by the Pennsylvanians; sour cream dressing was another notable contribution, along with corn salad (a favorite Amish dish), meat and egg salad, hot slaw, chestnut salad, horseradish salad, herring and apple salad, and oyster salad.

Relishes were one of the main things in which Pennsylvanian originality and inventiveness were shown to best advantage. As late as twenty-five or thirty years ago, and even today in rural districts, no housewife who had the slightest respect for herself would dream of asking her family, much less guests, to sit down to a table that didn't have at least the "seven sweets and seven sours" gracing the board. And each of these sweet and sour relishes was a triumph—rhubarb jam, rhubarb marmalade, lemon honey, cherry relish, pear marmalade, and quince marmalade were the most unusual "sweets," but all the standard preserves were served from time to time as well. The "sours" included such dishes as green tomato relish, cucumber relish, onion, pepper, pickle relish, and vegetable catsup.

These relishes and preserves would not be the only bottles or jars on the shelves of the average pantry. Each year energetic housewives put up huge quantities of vegetables and added these to the stores of dried fruits. Usually a family had enough food on hand to supply a small community for several months at a time, and each family was almost entirely self-sufficient and independent.

Baking day is the occasion remembered perhaps more fondly than any other by Pennsylvanians who recall the old-time customs. And of all baking days, Fastnacht Day, Shrove Tuesday (the last day before Lent begins), was the favorite. On that day, which was in ancient times a fast day—a custom long since completely abandoned by Pennsylvania Dutchmen —thousands and thousands of Fastnachts were baked, and still are in some parts of the state. This is a custom which might well be continued—especially in view of the fact that these doughnut-like treats are very good for dunking in coffee, or molasses, or both. Fastnachts were simply but carefully made of potatoes, flour, yeast, milk, butter, and sugar, left overnight to rise, and fried in deep fat.

Not only in these, but in many other pastries and

cakes the Pennsylvanians surpassed themselves. Eggs were used extensively both in cooking and for omelets, but it was in thickly iced cakes, rich pies, and cookies that the egg was most frequently glorified. This, together with the excellence of the quality of the lard used, practically insured success for every cook's efforts.

There would be plenty of huge layer cakes on every table at meal time. Or possibly there'd be shoofly pie—this particular Dutch sweet was about the size of an average cake and well-deserved its name, for rich, gooey molasses oozed from its tiny pores, making it a definite attraction to hungry boys and miscellaneous adventurous flies. However, Pennsylvania's housewives were so carefully tidy and clean it is doubtful that the flies very often got this opportunity.

Another small-boy favorite was "funny cake," which started out to be a chocolate pie and ended up having plain cake dough poured over it just before it was baked. Pennsylvania cinnamon buns, too, were probably the biggest and best the world has ever known. Big and raisin-filled, these had scant resemblance to their commercial descendants of today.

Buttered noodles were an early favorite, as were potato dumplings, onion gravy, apple butter, horseradish gravy, spiced pot-roast, pork and kraut,

Hasenpfeffer (rabbit stew), clam omelet, and pickled eggs. These are a few of the typical Dutch dishes that were either developed entirely by Pennsylvanians or improved upon considerably by them.

There are inns in Pennsylvania today—comfortable, well-aged, and mellow spots—where meals are still served in the former lavish fashion, where leisurely waitresses still produce a huge, delicious dinner that presents three serious problems to the modern diner—what to choose, how to save room for dessert, and how to become accustomed to ordinary cooking again. And in the countrysides around Bethlehem, Allentown, Lancaster, and many other cities, families still gather to such a table as delighted the Historical Society.

For food to the Pennsylvanians was a challenge, an urge to use more skill, more ideas, and more cunning in preparing it, and this talent and attitude has never been forgotten. Food was also a pastime—a basis for hospitality—a pledge of friendship. Food was a very present help in time of trouble as well. In the country it was the custom for mourners to repair to the home of the deceased immediately after the funeral for an immense feast. For miles around, tramps and hobos would gather to pay their respects and enjoy the huge meal relatives had been two days in preparing. Oftentimes, a table would be set at noon for as many people as could be seated at it, and at six o'clock people would still be eating.

All in all, the Pennsylvania Dutch have clung to their customs, and one of their happiest habits is the cooking and eating of delicious foods. Their knowledge and skill has been handed on to thousands of people in other states. It is a heritage of their descendants in Pennsylvania, where today the standard of cooking simply but well is still the criterion for a good housewife.

TO BELIEVE IN WITCHCRAFT

A BELIEF in witchcraft lingers here and there in the dark places of the Pennsylvania countryside. The various racial elements that settled in the state brought from the Old World big ancestral cargoes of superstitions and legends, some of which persist to-day. These ancient beliefs exist alongside orthodox religion and have been preserved by the people as part of their living traditions. Powwow doctors still repeat magic formulae to bring desired results to pass; but as a career for the young the practice of the Black Art can hardly be recommended, even though · to become a practitioner it is unnecessary to serve an apprenticeship, or graduate from a school for witch doctors, or pass an examination for a license. Truth to tell, there is scarcely enough business to make it worthwhile.

Pennsylvania has always prided itself on the fact that when the sport of witch hunting was at full throttle in New England only one case occurred in Philadelphia, and the alleged witches—two Swedish women—were freed. William Penn himself charged the jury, which found that while the defendants were guilty of having the reputation of witches, they were not guilty as charged of any overt acts of witchcraft. In one respect the proceedings followed the usual pattern of such trials in New England and elsewhere. The statement of the daughter of one of the women that her mother was a witch was admitted in evidence. The part that mischievous children and young people played in these trials, sometimes sending their own parents to the gallows, is one of the most amazing things about them.

Since those early days Pennsylvania rather than New England has become the witchcraft center of the country. Pennsylvanians blame New Englanders for being to some extent responsible for pinning this reputation on the commonwealth. Wallace

Nutting is charged with first printing the story that the symbols painted on barns in the Dutch country are hex marks superstitiously employed to ward off witches, who take special delight in putting their necromancy on cattle. In his *Pennsylvania Beautiful*, published in 1924, Nutting mentions these *hexefuss* as being a continuance of a very ancient tradition and remarks on their being a simpler and more humane measure against witches than the violent ones adopted by New England. The Germans insist that these bulls'-eyes are purely decorative.

Another New Englander, who was at one time Superintendent of Public Instruction in Pennsylvania, is likewise charged with statements calculated to give the state a bad name for superstition and ignorance. During Governor Earle's administration the following news item appeared in a Harrisburg paper.

"State educators declared here yesterday that hexerei, terror of numerous rural farm communities for many years, is being banished from Pennsylvania by the public schools.

"School authorities explained that instruction in the sciences, even in the lower grades, has proved the most effective weapon against the superstition.

"They say that hex symbols calculated to cause illness in a farmhouse or disease of cattle still may be seen on barns and houses, but that younger rural folk spurn beliefs that frightened their kin a few years back.

"Court records show the hex responsible for many crimes, including murder and arson, during the past 50 years."

Some Pennsylvania writers approach the subject of witchcraft as if it were a Bluebeard cupboard which on no account should be looked into, lest something discreditable to the state should be revealed, and so they bypass it. But A. Monroe Aurand, Jr., of Harrisburg, from whose work on witchcraft the foregoing quotation has been taken, has not hesitated to investigate and ventilate the whole business. His conclusion is that witchcraft today in Pennsylvania can hardly be said to assume the nature of a peril. Superstitions exist, but no more so here than elsewhere in the country. And Professor George Lyman Kittredge of Harvard, writing to Mr. Aurand, said, "You are quite right in thinking that Pennsylvania should not be particularly discredited on account of the belief in witches. That belief is our inheritance from very ancient times; and, in my opinion, is still held, in some form or other, by nine-tenths of the human race."

The Pennsylvania Germans have been singled out as being more addicted to superstitious fears and practices than other folk. John Kelpius, the Hermit of the Wissahickon, who came over with his followers in 1694, was viewed with suspicion by the Quakers because he was evidently a believer in alchemy. He owned a wisdom stone which just before his death he threw into the Wissahickon. Careful search was made for the magic pebble, but it was never found. In Morse's *American Geography*, published in 1789, it is said of the Pennsylvania Germans, "The lower class are very ignorant and superstitious. It is not uncommon to see them going to market with a little bag of salt tied to their horses' manes, for the purpose, they say, of keeping off witches." The German language press of Pennsylvania during the eighteenth century did its best to stamp out superstition among the Germans. But even today those who deny that the symbols on barns have any supernatural significance admit that the triangles cut into the lintels of barns are genuine hex marks. The Pennsylvania Germans have maintained with unflinching conservatism the traditional ways, manners, and speech which have been handed down generation after generation by their forefathers. Many of them originally came from a section of Middle Europe that was a particularly fertile field for fabulous stories and legends, and if some of them still cherish a few old and queer beliefs one cannot quarrel with them.

Belief in witchcraft, however, is by no means confined to the Germans in Pennsylvania. The other day I talked with a man of Welsh descent who was reared on a farm between the mountains of Fulton County, which is on the Mason and Dixon line halfway across the state. There are few Germans here and not a single mile of railroad in the county. A line was once projected and construction actually begun, but this precipitated a railroad war. Men with rifles in the employ of rival transportation interests were posted on the hills to shoot at the wagons hauling dynamite from Maryland. The project was abandoned. The tunnels, which were all but completed, were not finished until years later when they were incorporated into the Pennsylvania Turnpike.

"My grandmother," said the Fulton County man, "would probably deny it because she has most likely forgotten, but, when the butter was hard to churn, I have seen her boil milk on the stove and jab it with a fork as she mumbled, 'Get out! Get out, and stay away!' "

"She thought it bewitched?" said I.

"Yes, she's a believer in spirits," he answered. "She believes that jack o'lanterns—the lights that glow along the mountains and disappear and come on again—are caused by spirits. There's some natural explanation, of course, but you couldn't convince my grandmother it was anything but spirits at work."

"What part of the county did she come from?"

"Toward the lower end," he said. "An out-of-the-way cove in the mountains. My grandfather used to say he didn't see how he ever got her out. He drove down in his farm wagon and brought her back, with her feather bed, her quilts, and some pieces of furniture that were hers. That was the way they did things in those days. My father and mother went to Bedford Springs on their honeymoon in a surrey with the fringe on top, a young colt running alongside the mare they were driving. My parents never took much stock in spirits, but there are still people besides my grandmother in Fulton county to whom they are very real."

Witchcraft has occasionally led to tragedy in Pennsylvania. Regrettable cases have arisen in which a mentally unbalanced person has become so obsessed with the idea he has been hexed that he has killed the person believed responsible for his bewitchment. Such was the Rehmeyer killing in York County in 1928, and the Shinsky murder near Pottsville in 1934.

In the former case, Nelson D. Rehmeyer, a sixty-year-old farmer, was killed by John H. Blymer, thirty-three, a former inmate of the State Hospital for the Insane, with the assistance of two boys, aged fourteen and eighteen. Blymer was seeking to break the spell which he believed Rehmeyer had put on him by getting from him a lock of hair or the pow-

wow book, *The Long Lost Friend*. The old man re-
sisted when the trio tried to throw and rope him, and
was killed in the fight.

Albert Shinsky claimed that his murder of Mrs.
Mummey, a "witch," was done in self-defense. Although Shinsky was twenty-three, he had the mind
of a child. "When I left his cell," said an examining
psychiatrist, "I knew I had been talking to an ado-
lescent boy of the most primitive development. I had
been talking with a mental and emotional infant."
Shinsky believed he was justified by the Bible in killing Mrs. Mummey. "He told me," said Warden William Watson of the Schuylkill County jail, "that
there are numerous instances in the Scriptures
where the sacrifice of human life has been declared
necessary." Albert, because obviously of unsound
mind, escaped paying the extreme penalty for the
Mummey murder, as did Blymer in the Rehmeyer
case.

These "witch" trials attracted so much attention
that some people got the impression that Pennsylvania had completely lost its soul. But such cases,
far from being a melancholy commonplace of contemporary Pennsylvania history, seldom occur,
though frequent attempts are made by the press to
tag cases untinctured by witchcraft with the hex
label. In this way the state has received bad marks
unjustly.

It's an Old Pennsylvania Custom

The notorious hex book, John George Hohman's *Pow-Wow; or the Long Lost Friend*, which figured in the Rehmeyer case, is the practice book used by all hex doctors of any pretensions. Originally published in German at Reading in 1820, it has since been translated and reissued many times. It is a witch's brew of ancient household remedies, incantations, and charms largely cribbed by Hohman from a medieval work by Albertus Magnus entitled *Egyptian Secrets of White and Black Magic*. To cure hysteria, for example, the hex doctor places the joint of his thumb on the bare flesh over the patient's heart and says, "Matrix, patrix, lay thyself right and safe, or thou and I shall on the third day fill the grave." If you have a persecution complex, wicked or malicious persons can be prevented from doing you an injury with this formula: "Dullix, ix, ux. Yes, you can't come over Pontio; Pontio is above Pilato." If you are down in the mouth because you have had bad luck at cards, "Tie the heart of a bat with a red silken string to the right arm, and you will win every game at cards you play." Mr. Hohman tells not only how to cure warts and snake bites, but how to treat various ailments of horses, cattle, and sheep. Information on how to make divinatory wands and beer is included, with instructions on how to spellbind a thief, catch fish, and prevent cherries from becoming ripe before Martinmas.

The hex doctors of Pennsylvania, now a diminishing band, are faith healers, and their incantations have doubtless given relief in cases where the trouble existed chiefly in the mind of the patient. Danger has arisen in cases where something more than simple abracadabra was needed. A few years ago there was the case of the Lebanon girl whose three-months-old baby died of malnutrition because she persisted in employing a hex doctor instead of a regular physician. The girl believed implicitly in the power of the hex doctor to help her baby.

A cat figured in the Shinsky case, but, strange to say, there seems to be no mention of cats in Dr. Hohman's *Hexbuch*. It is a curious omission, as cats have for centuries been commonly associated with witches. "Thrice the brindled cat hath mew'd." It is very usual for witches to take the form of a black cat, in which disguise they glide darkly about their diabolical business. It is an old Pennsylvania saying, "When a witch disappears, a black cat appears." Black cats everywhere are considered creatures of ill omen, and few persons are pleased to have them cross their path. During the summer of 1797 vast numbers of Philadelphia cats suddenly and mysteriously died. They were found dead all over the place —in the streets and alleys, on doorsteps and by hearthsides. Cats of all colors from white to Quaker gray and black perished miserably, and no one has ever been able to explain it.

But we need not pursue the subject any further. Superstitions prevail everywhere, among civilized and savage races alike, but not unduly in Pennsylvania. Occasionally insanely credulous persons may be found who insist that there are such things as witches, but not many of these people live in Pennsylvania.

TO OBSERVE STRANGE CUSTOMS OF
COURTSHIP AND MARRIAGE

MARRIAGE used to be a lottery among the Moravians of Pennsylvania. In 1756, when Benjamin Franklin was employed on the frontier building forts, he stopped at the town of Bethlehem, where, being a man of rewarding curiosity, he asked the Germans about their peculiar marriage customs.

"I inquired concerning the Moravian marriages," he says in his *Autobiography*, "whether the report was true that they were by lot. I was told that lots were used only in particular cases; that generally, when a young man found himself disposed to marry, he informed the elders of his class, who consulted the elder ladies that governed the young women. As these elders of the different sexes were well acquainted with the tempers and dispositions of their respective pupils, they could best judge what matches were suitable, and their judgments were generally acquiesced in. But if, for example, it should happen that two or three young women were found to be equally proper for the young man, the lot was then recurred to. I objected, if the matches are not made by the mutual choice of the parties, some of them may chance to be very unhappy. 'And so they may,' answered my informer, 'if you let the parties choose for themselves.' Which indeed I could not deny."

According to another account, the Moravians believed all matches were made in heaven. A register was kept by the society of all marriageable persons of both sexes, and, whenever a candidate for matrimony presented himself, a number of ballots with the names of all unmarried females were placed in a box from which the trembling young man was allowed to draw. If he happened to draw the desired name, all was merry as a marriage bell, but if either party refused to "solemnize," the objector was thrown off the register for a term of years, after which the experiment could be tried again. This method of choosing a mate by lot did away, of course, with all the pleasant preliminaries of courtship. There were no lovers' quarrels and reconciliations, none of that sweet madness.

A feature of all Moravian villages was the Brothers' house and the Sisters' house, where those who preferred the single life could live. These houses were also havens for those who were unlucky in the matrimonial lottery. At Moravian weddings pretzels and wine were served.

One of the most delightful customs associated with courtship and marriage in Pennsylvania is that of the Amish blue gate. Anyone who drives through the Dutch country where there are Amish communities must in time notice the prevalence of blue fence gates before the solid, neat houses. When an Amish girl reaches marriageable age a debutante party is not given for her, but the front gate is painted blue. In this way are the attentions of eligible young men invited. The Amish themselves smilingly deny the story, saying it is unnecessary for them to do this in order to marry off their daughters. But the legend persists, and the Amish shake their heads at the queer ways of the people about them—and continue to paint their gates blue because that happens to be their favorite color.

Since these people have no use for automobiles,

young Amishmen go courting as all young men did in the horse-and-buggy age. On reaching the age of romance each is customarily provided with a good horse, a new harness, and a new topless buggy. In this old-fashioned rig he calls on his girl and takes her out riding. After marriage he may use a top-buggy when driving his wife, but in no case is he permitted to have a buggy with a dashboard.

The ancient custom of bundling, which is commonly thought to have been practiced only in chill New England, had a long run in Pennsylvania, where it was very popular among the Germans. Social historians, indeed, say that the custom lingered longer in Pennsylvania than anywhere else, and some persons insist that it is not yet dead. But it is doubtful if any sizable group still practices this method of courtship.

An Amish wedding is an all-day affair. It customarily takes place in the fall after the harvest has been taken care of and before winter sets in, the weeks immediately preceding and following Thanksgiving being the most popular. The ceremony begins at an early hour of the morning and as several ministers and deacons speak at length is rarely concluded before noon. This is the most solemn occasion in the life of an Amish man or woman, and the service is conducted with extraordinary dignity and impressiveness. After the ceremony the whole group sits down to a gargantuan wedding feast—dozens of fowl, great platters of meats, heaps of cakes and cookies, scores of pies. The banquet, which is as gay as the morning service is solemn, lasts well into the afternoon, and the tables have hardly been cleared when supper is served. In the evening, while the older folk sit discussing crops and agricultural problems, the young people sing and play games. Some time during the evening the bridegroom is caught up by his friends and tossed over the nearest fence. And having observed this tradition, the guests consider the marriage final. Final it is, too. There is no divorce among the Amish and rarely a separation, for among the plain people a contract once made holds good forever.

Quaker weddings are perhaps the simplest of all. No words are wasted, scarcely more than the bare minimum to fulfill the legal requirements being used. The rest is silence. Yet in its frugality of words and simplicity the Quaker ritual is a deeply impressive one.

Preserved in Sherman Day's *Historical Collections of Pennsylvania* is an interesting old account of a frontier wedding. This was an event the whole community looked forward to eagerly, because it was almost the only social gathering that did not involve some form of labor, such as harvesting, logrolling, or house raising.

On the day of the wedding the groom and his attendants, his relatives, and friends, gathered at his father's house early enough in the morning to enable them to reach the bride's home by noon, the customary time for the ceremony. "Let the reader imagine an assemblage of persons," says the account quoted by Day, "without a store, tailor, or mantuamaker within a hundred miles; and an assemblage of horses, without a blacksmith or saddler within an equal distance. The gentlemen dressed in shoe-packs, moccasins, leather breeches, leggings, linsey hunting-shirts, and all home-made. The ladies dressed in linsey petticoats, and linsey or linen bedgowns, coarse shoes, stockings, handkerchiefs, and buckskin gloves, if any. If there were any buckles, rings, buttons, or ruffles, they were the relics of old times; family pieces from parents or grandparents. The horses were caparisoned with old saddles, old bridles or halters, and packsaddles, with a bag or blanket thrown over them; a rope or string as often constituted the girth, as a piece of leather."

The procession in double file was often interrupted by the narrowness and obstructions of the horse paths, as they were called, for there were no roads; and these difficulties were often increased, sometimes by the good will and sometimes by the ill will of neighbors, who felled trees and tied grapevines across the way. Sometimes an ambuscade was formed by the wayside, and an unexpected discharge of several guns took place, covering the wedding party with smoke. "Let the reader imagine the scene which followed this discharge; the sudden spring of the horses, the shrieks of the girls, and the chivalric bustle of their partners to save them from falling. Sometimes, in spite of all that could be done to prevent it, some were thrown to the ground. If a wrist, elbow, or ankle happened to be sprained, it was tied with a handkerchief, and little more was thought or said about it."

Before the backwoods cavalcade reached the bride's house, a ceremony called the race for the bottle was customarily observed. When the party reached a point about a mile from its destination, two young men were singled out to ride for the whisky, and the worse the path, the more logs, muddy hollows, brush, and other obstacles, the better, because these gave the contestants a greater opportunity to show their daring and skill in horsemanship. Fraught with danger to both horses and riders, the race started with an Indian yell, and the first rider to reach the door of the bride's house was given Black Betty, the prize bottle of whisky, which was always filled for the occasion. Acknowledging it with a whoop, the rider wheeled and tore back in triumph to the advancing troop, to which he announced his victory with another yell. The groom, at the head of the procession, got the first drink, his attendants came next, and then each pair in turn to the end of the line. The prize winner then stowed Black Betty in the bosom of his hunting shirt and took his place in the cavalcade.

Following the marriage ceremony, the whole company partook of the wedding feast. Prodigious quantities of provender were provided for the guests —beef, pork, and fowls, roasted and boiled, and sometimes venison and bear meat, accompanied by a variety of other viands in generous measure. "During the dinner the greatest hilarity always prevailed, although the table might be a large slab of timber, hewed out with a broadaxe, supported by four sticks set in auger holes; and the furniture, some old pewter dishes and plates; the rest, wooden bowls and trenchers; a few pewter spoons, much battered about the edges, were to be seen at some tables. The rest were made of horns. If knives were scarce, the deficiency was made up by the scalping-knives, which were carried in sheaths suspended from the belt of the hunting shirt."

With dinner over, the place was immediately cleared for dancing, and the fiddler, by this time feeling at concert pitch, went into action. It was real dancing, too, joyous and spontaneous; jigs, reels, and square sets. It continued all night. "The commencement was always a square four, which was followed by what was called jigging it off; that is, two of the four would single out for a jig, and were followed by the remaining couple. The jigs were often accompanied with what was called cutting out; that is, when either of the parties became tired of the dance, on intimation the place was supplied by some one of the company without any interruption of the dance. In this way a dance was often continued till the musician was heartily tired of his situation. Toward the latter part of the night, if any of the company, through weariness, attempted to conceal themselves, for the purpose of sleeping, they were hunted up, paraded on the floor, and the fiddler ordered to play *Hang Out Till Tomorrow Morning.*" The backwoods fiddlers, like the country fiddlers of today, held their violins on their arms, not under their chins.

"About nine or ten o'clock," the account continues, "a deputation of the young ladies stole off the bride, and put her to bed. In doing this, it frequently happened that they had to ascend a ladder instead of a pair of stairs, leading from the dining and ball-rooms to the loft, the floor of which was made of clapboards, lying loose and without nails. As the foot of the ladder was commonly behind the door, which was purposely opened for the occasion, and its rounds at the inner ends were well hung with hunting shirts, petticoats, and other articles of clothing, the candles being on the opposite side of the house, the exit of the bride was noticed by but few.

"This done, a deputation of young men in like manner stole off the groom, and placed him snugly by the side of his bride. The dance still continued; and if seats happened to be scarce, which was often the case, every young man, when not engaged in the dance was obliged to offer his lap as a seat for one of the girls; and the offer was sure to be accepted. In the midst of this hilarity the bride and groom were not forgotten. Pretty late in the night, someone would remind the company that the new couple must stand in need of some refreshment; Black Betty was called for and sent up the ladder but sometimes Black Betty did not go alone. I have many times seen as much bread, beef, pork, and cabbage, sent along with her, as would afford a good meal for half a dozen hungry men. The young couple were compelled to eat and drink, more or less, of whatever was offered them."

On the homeward trek the order of procession was the same as before, and the race through brush and briar for Black Betty was repeated at the other end. The horses as well as the members of the party were likely to bear marks of the frolic on which they had been. For it often happened that neighbors and relatives who were not asked to the wedding showed their resentment by cutting off the manes, foretops, and tails, of the horses.

The feasting and dancing at these backwoods weddings and at the infare that followed frequently lasted for several days, until "the whole company were so exhausted with loss of sleep that several days' rest were requisite to fit them to return to their ordinary labors."

When Chester County established a poor farm on the banks of the Brandywine in 1798, it was faced with an unexpected problem of courtship and marriage. The number of inmates which was at first 118 rose at an alarming rate. "Too free an intercourse was permitted among the inmates; frequent marriages took place among the paupers, and the county family was found to increase more rapidly than was prudent for the best interests of the county, or the comfort and good morals of the establishment; and better regulations were consequently introduced," says a local historian of those days.

TO WEAR BEARDS AND
DRESS PLAINLY

PENNSYLVANIA can boast of having more
bearded men than any state in the Union, thanks
to the presence within its borders of certain religious
groups that wear the beard as a matter of principle.
The Amish people in particular, who are largely
centered in Lancaster County, the heart of the Dutch
country, are noted for their beards. These religionists have for centuries kept faith with the tradition
of the valanced face, and on market days, when the

Amish farmers come to town in force, the city of Lancaster is cloudy with beards.

Before they are married or join the church, Amishmen are clean-shaven, but when they become legally mated they let their beards grow, so that the bachelors, the newly wedded, and those who have for some time enjoyed the marital status, are usually easily recognizable by the absence or presence of a beard and whether it is partly or fully grown. But married or single, none ever wears a mustache. To prevent interference with taking the sacrament and receiving and bestowing the sacred kiss and for convenience in eating, the upper lip is religiously reaped.

They wear their hair long, too, though trimming is permissible and they seldom look unkempt. The hair is usually cut in an even bang across the forehead, combed down and docked all around on a line with the ears in a so-called Dutch cut. The utmost care has to be taken not to clip either the hair or the beard too short, because, if the cutting is overdone, the transgressor is visited with the discipline of the church, which is something to be avoided. All tonsorial work is done in the home, never in a barbershop, for these people have as little use for barbers as they have for lawyers. These two traditionally wordy professions are practically under an Amish ban.

Amishmen's hair and beards seem always the same color, says A. Monroe Aurand, Jr., the Harrisburg author, publisher, and bookseller. Sandy verging on red is the dominant shade. Many have fine old port-drinking complexions that go well with their reddish whiskers, but as they are a very temperate people this facial hue must be attributed to something besides drinking. In view of the Amish liking for blue, it is a pity that the jetty beard with bluish glints in it, such as that which gave the notorious Gilles des Rais his nickname of Bluebeard, is practically nonexistent among these splendidly hirsute people.

The women wear their hair in the simplest style. No upsweeps, no page-boy cuts, no permanents. It is parted in the middle, combed down smoothly on either side, brought around in two plaits, and knotted at the back. Parting on the side is expressly forbidden to women as well as to men, and naturally there are no curls and no ornaments. At home or abroad, indoors or out, the Amish woman wears over the knot or bun at the back of her head a small white cap, for it is plainly written in the Scripture that a "woman that prayeth or prophesieth with her head uncovered dishonoreth her head."

Their dress is the most distinctive characteristic of these simple folk. To the casual visitor who sees them for the first time as they come to town on market day, it must seem that they have stepped out of a centuries-old picture. And indeed they might have done just that, so little have their garments changed since the sect was founded in the seventeenth century in Switzerland. The same is more or less true of all the "plain" sects, but of all these pietists the disciples of Ammon have been most strict.

The Amish group is historically a branch of the Mennonite movement, which in turn had its source in the great Anabaptist upsurge of the sixteenth century. In 1693 one of the leaders of the movement, Jacob Ammon, withdrew, feeling that the teachings of the founder, Menno Simons, were being too loosely enforced. Ammon appears to have been a man cut from the cloth of the Old Testament prophets. He spoke with the voice of doom and authority, and demanded and received from his small band of followers the utmost in obedience. It was he who established the rules that constitute the basis of Amish society even down to the present.

Among other things, Ammon fixed the style of dress which persists to this day. As a special mark of devotion to the cause, he introduced "plain" dress and demanded that, in place of buttons, which suggested military uniforms to the pacifist Amish, hooks and eyes be substituted on clothing. He thundered against ornamentation and denounced the frivolity and pride which led men to decorate their clothing with such frills and fancies as buttons. He set the style in clothing, hats, shoes, and coiffure, and darkly warned that those who persisted in evil and worldly ways would inevitably come under the shadow of excommunication. His stern guidance in matters of dress and theology was so firmly imbedded in the Amish mind that the Amishman in the Lancaster market today is almost an exact reflection of Ammon himself. Cruelly persecuted in Europe, driven at last to seek safety and freedom in the most liberal of colonies, they have walled themselves, Chinese-like, within their communities and wear the badge of their convictions as proudly as did their founder.

The broad-brimmed, low-crowned hat is still worn, varied only in summer with straw headgear of the same pattern. The men's coats of plain cloth have no lapels and are devoid of buttons and outside pockets. Like their high vests, they are fastened with the traditional hooks and eyes. Their trousers open on either side near the seams and because of the wide front flap are called "front fall" or "broad fall." Their shirts may be of plain solid colors, but never patterned. Overcoats are long, dark, and voluminous, and are frequently topped with a heavy broad cape. Caps, belts, ties, and other articles of haberdashery are all scorned as unnecessary adornments. Disputes have even arisen about the propriety of wearing plain home-made suspenders, and at one time reached such a pitch that a one-suspender, middle-of-the-road group set itself up as a separate unit. But whatever differences may occasionally arise, the firm stand against the button remains universal among the Amish. "What," say they, "are buttons, but a place for the devil to catch on?"

The women dress more plainly, if anything, than the men. Their full, dark skirts come well down over the tops of their high black shoes. Their dresses need not always be funeral black but may be of a sober soft hue, most commonly blue and less frequently purple or green. Over their shoulders they almost invariably wear a cape or shawl fastened at the neck and falling to the waist back and front. The most characteristic feature of the Amish women's dress is, of course, the bonnet. This comes well over the face and is fashioned of black or gray cloth over a curved stiffening. It is full enough at the back to reach the shoulders and is tied demurely under the chin.

From the time they learn to walk the children are dressed like miniature adults, the boys in broad-brimmed hats and long trousers, the girls in full, ankle-length dresses. The sober, plain dress contrasts oddly with their bright childish faces, and to watch them at their games in the school yard is to see playful little old men and women come to life from some half-remembered story book.

To the observer the Amish dress seems so outlandish that the thought inevitably arises that here must be a people bent on making themselves conspicuous. Actually, the reverse is more nearly true, for the Amish have merely avoided the modernity which to them is shocking and frivolous display. They have clung tenaciously to the plain and serviceable garb of their people, while others have sought after the queer, the modish, the proud, and the revealing. They are true conservatives, firmly convinced of the righteousness of their ways and happy to demonstrate their convictions daily in their dress and customs.

The folkways of the Amish are tenaciously and lovingly preserved. Perhaps the most effective barrier they have hedged themselves with is that of language, for the Pennsylvania Dutch they speak is a unique and exclusive dialect. They originally spoke German, but, cut off from contact with the main stream of the language, the dialect has taken on an archaic flavor and rhythm unknown elsewhere. The vocabulary itself contains much that has long since been dropped from German and is at the same time colored with many borrowed words and phrases. Though the Amish dialect is understood generally throughout the area by those of German extraction, it is extremely difficult, if not unintelligible, to outsiders. The odd sing-song rhythm and the upward inflection of phrases and sentences give it a purely local color. The children learn to speak this dialect first, and, though they are taught English at school, it is common for the first graders to be completely bewildered by the new language when first subjected to it. At the same time they are taught to read High German at home, for church services are conducted not in the dialect but in a purer form of the language. But even though they must be familiar with both English and German, the Amish people prefer to use their own Pennsylvania Dutch, for it serves admirably to exclude people and ideas which would sweep them along in the worldly ways of today.

In following the customs of their fathers and fathers' fathers the Amish feel they are achieving God's purposes and their own salvation. Primarily they are obeying implicitly the scriptural law laid down for the guidance of man. Such was the purpose of Ammon and such has been the endeavor of his followers since then. In all things they live a Christian life according to their tenets, obeying Biblical law in a direct, primitive, fundamentalist sense. As far as possible they ignore the man-made laws of the state. They hold no high office, vote only in local elections if at all, receive no aid from government agencies, and have no resort to the courts but handle their own problems and settle in their own church communities whatever disputes may arise among them. They believe firmly and immovably in non-resistance, accept vilification, abuse, or the most menial task assigned to the conscientious objector with unwavering stolidity. Though they refuse to bear arms in war, they have invested in bonds the proceeds of which went to nonmilitary activities and they have contributed handsomely to the relief of suffering among all people.

In all things they live according to the dictates of their conscience and in conformity with Biblical injunctions. Man, they believe, was created to multiply and subdue the earth. They are, therefore, farmers, and to this calling they devote their whole strength. They work the land carefully and lovingly. The worn-out lands they occupied generations ago have been brought back to fertility by their industry and prudence. In the earliest times they practiced crop rotation and replenishment of the soil while others were sapping its strength, and today their fields and homes can be distinguished easily by the most unpracticed observer.

Education beyond the fundamentals necessary to their simple life they look upon as a waste and a danger. Learning beyond what is useful can only be a temptation, and whenever possible they have tried to limit formal schooling to the eighth grade and to keep their children closely within their own Amish communities. With the consolidation of the rural schools in recent years, they have obtained permission to establish their own parochial schools. None of their people go on to enter the professions, though they have no objections to others entering these fields and, in fact, are ready to use the services of specialists of all sorts whenever they may be needed. They are not particularly superstitious people, though among them, as among all groups, there are those given to odd beliefs, such as pow-wowism for healing.

The simple life, uncomplicated by modern devices not mentioned in Holy Writ, remains their goal. The telephone, the radio, the automobile, the tractor, the furnace, the can-opener—all are unwanted. Their houses are comfortable, though unadorned with fancy furniture, curtains, refrigerators, or door bells. The Bible forbids the making of graven images, and the Amish accordingly avoid photographs, paintings, and art work of all kinds.

Even their religious services are of the plainest sort. In his *History and Customs of the Amish People,* H. M. J. Klein describes in detail the mood and manner of the Amish meetings. They are held in rotation in the homes of the members, and the rooms are ordinarily arranged so that wide doors may be opened between them to accommodate a considerable number. Since chairs are not used, except by the old and feeble, wooden benches are brought in and the women arrange themselves in one room and the men in another. The minister who conducts the meeting is one of their neighbors, a man with no special training. He, as well as all the bishops and deacons, is selected by lot, and it is assumed that God will provide the skill and eloquence needed to carry on His work. There are usually two sermons delivered, a brief one and a longer, more formal one, and the men who are to deliver them are chosen while the opening hymn is being sung.

The singing is extremely interesting. The hymns themselves are hallowed by long use and known to every worshiper. Most of them come from a hymnal called the *Ausbund*, which is thought to be the oldest book of its kind in America. Many of the songs it contains were written before 1600, and the melodies, which are sung without accompaniment, are said to bear a striking resemblance to the Gregorian chants.

But with all their sternness and sobriety, the Amish are not a grim folk. They are warm and generous and, among themselves, at least, convivial and talkative. There is little in their make-up of the brooding sense of doom commonly associated with the Puritans, but rather an air of enjoyment and fulfillment in their dedication. They are hearty in **their pleasure and participate freely in community** functions and entertainments—barn raisings, husking bees, quilting parties, auction sales, market days. In the field and in the house, they work hard and long, but when the day's work is finished they have both the time and inclination for wholesome recreation. Sufficient unto themselves, a segment of society apparently transplanted whole from a forgotten era, these bearded, plainly dressed folk labor quietly in their vineyards and prosper in the respect of their neighbors.

TO EMBELLISH THE USEFUL

ONE of the most interesting manifestations of popular and traditional art in America is the rich and colorful vein of self-expression displayed by the Pennsylvania Germans. Here was a homogeneous people who were so clannish and conservative in their attachment to their own traditions that they succeeded in transplanting to Pennsylvania not only their religion and language but their quaint customs and art as well.

To Embellish the Useful

Although the United States stands well ahead of many countries in the appreciation of popular art, it is not so many years ago that this interest first began to manifest itself. In 1891, when the late Dr. Edwin Atlee Barber, curator of the Pennsylvania Museum of Fine Arts, began to assemble that institution's notable collection of ceramics from the Dutch countryside, hardly a ripple of interest was aroused. Since then, however, knowledge of and interest in the distinctive arts of the Pennsylvania Germans has spread far and wide. Several rooms in the American Wing of the Metropolitan Museum of Art in New York are devoted to a permanent display of objects from the eastern counties—gaily decorated dower chests, furniture of all kinds, wood carvings, earthenware, cast iron and wrought iron, glass, fractur work, needle work, an inlaid Kentucky rifle, etc. The craze for antiques in the nineteen-twenties caused a surge of enthusiasm for Pennsylvania Dutch heirlooms which had been largely overlooked by collectors. The popularity of peasant art imported in vast quantities from foreign lands heightened interest in the arts and crafts of Pennsylvania.

It is always possible to tell when you are in the Dutch country by the neatness of the farms and the great barns that dominate each collection of buildings. The German influence is also noticeable in some of the older towns, which are laid out like those of Saxony in central Germany and some of those in northern Germany. They are entered through narrow ways and then open up into a cobbled or paved square, with perhaps high-shouldered houses standing about, their steeply-pitched roofs slanting toward the street. And while in the Pennsylvania towns settled by New Englanders there is a preponderance of white houses, the Germans loved to paint their towns red.

Among the interesting examples of folk art preserved and practiced by the Pennsylvania Germans was their fractur work, or the art of illuminated writing, which was highly popular with them for the best part of two centuries, particularly in the form of birth and baptismal certificates, marriage certificates, and to a lesser degree death certificates. The name *Fraktur-schriften*, to use the German term, comes from a sixteenth-century German printing type called *Fraktur*, which bore a strong family resemblance to the script used at that time by the engrossers of documents and manuscripts. The Pennsylvania calligraphers did not, however, slavishly follow this type face, but indulged their own ideas and developed some very curious and beautiful writing which, combined with brilliantly colored floral borders and drawings of birds, beasts, men, and angels, often resulted in the most delightful artistic effects.

Appropriately enough, this medieval art fostered by the monasteries of Europe flourished at the Ephrata Cloisters in Pennsylvania, where the walls were covered with large sheets of fractur work, many of them framed scriptural texts or pious sentiments in praise of celibacy and the cloistered life. These were executed on paper manufactured expressly for the purpose in the paper mill of the sect. Books, especially the hymn books used by these religionists, were multiplied in manuscript and illuminated by the sisters, who also produced by hand *The Christian A B C Book* (1750), a lettering book for fractur writers, containing a number of highly decorative alphabets.

To teach their pupils to write, it was a custom of schoolmasters to draw up what was called a *Vorschrift*, or sampler of letters, some of which are beautiful specimens of penmanship.

Most of the fractur work was done by clergymen and schoolmasters—especially the latter—who prided themselves on their writing and decorative abilities and were glad to eke out their beggarly pay with the extra money they could pick up by fractur writing. This took the form not only of birth and baptismal certificates, but house mottoes or blessings, bookplates and bookmarkers, and the embellishment of genealogical records in family Bibles and title pages in song books. All were richly illuminated with homemade colored inks applied with quill and brush. What the artist lacked in draughtsmanship he made up for by the extravagant use of color. Even when it became possible to buy printed certificates which the scrivener filled in, he was not content merely to write in names and dates, but usually added decorations of his own to the printed form. The certificates were framed and hung on the walls, and the more elaborate and colorful they were the better people liked them.

If a fractur writer hit upon a design he thought especially good or which struck the popular fancy in the theater of his operations, he did not hesitate to use it again and again, in the same way that decorators of dower chests repeated themselves. But there was scarcely a neighborhood without its fractur writer, so the certificates that have survived show infinite variety. They are mostly the work, good, bad, and indifferent, of anonymous penmen.

The designs incorporated hearts and flowers, usually in a connected growth or frame with birds perched in the foliage. As in the case of everything the Pennsylvania Germans decorated, the tulip was the principal flower used. The birds included turtle doves, parrots, peacocks, pelicans, humming birds, double-headed eagles, and roosters. Because the designs were at first based on remembered art from the country of their origin, the German fractur writers employed heraldic lions, unicorns, and stags. Horses, often with riders, frequently appear. Angels and mermaids were popular. Barn symbols and crowns commonly formed part of the design.

Fractur writing became a trade pursued by artists who wandered about the countryside in summer and worked the towns in the winter. Like the peddlers, they became acquainted with the people and seemed to know when their services would be required. But customs have their entrances and exits, and toward the close of the last century the demand for illuminated certificates slackened. The last itinerant fractur writer carried on into the present century, according to Frances Lichen (*Folk Art of Rural Pennsylvania*), but when he died the custom passed away with him.

The German pioneers brought very few household utensils with them when they came to this country, but there were numerous trades represented among them, including that of the potters, who very early in the history of the settlements began to make all kinds of earthenware to meet the needs of housewives. Fortunately, suitable clay for the purpose was easily obtainable in the districts where they settled, and the potters turned out quantities of plates, bowls, pots, crocks, mugs, and other articles, to say nothing of roof tiles. The local clay used came out of the kilns, after firing, a reddish-brown color; hence the name Pennsylvania red-ware.

By far the commonest article made by the Pennsylvania potters was the pie plate or *poi-schissel*, a simple, curved baking dish. In their love for and consumption of pie the Pennsylvania Germans surpassed the New Englanders. Fruit pies were especially popular with them, and these and other varieties were baked in the spacious outdoor Dutch ovens in batches never dreamed of in the philosophy of a New England housewife. Making pies in great numbers required stacks of plates. Different sizes were used. The pie plate output of the potteries, accordingly, was enormous.

The German potters decorated practically everything they produced, even pie plates, using either one of two modes, sometimes both, namely, slip decoration and sgraffito. To slip-decorate a plate, the potter took a plate that had just been molded but not fired and, with a cup of liquid clay equipped with a quill through which the clay flowed in a tiny stream, he worked out his design on the surface of the plate. Sometimes he used a cup equipped with several quills which enabled him to produce two or three lines simultaneously. Different colored clays were used in slip-covering plates and other pieces of earthenware.

Sgraffito decoration was done by covering a plate or other object of redware with a thin coating of white clay and etching the design in this deeply enough to disclose the red beneath the white. Other colors could be added with a slip cup. Plates decorated in this way were for ornament rather than everyday use and were highly prized by their owners. Many of the potters were masters of design. Patterns of flowers, birds, animals, and human figures appear on their plates. Sometimes a wise or humorous saying in German was used as a border. Much of this work was done free hand.

Potteries in England made a direct bid for Pennsylvania German patronage by making china decorated to their taste in a style called "gaudy Dutch." Tulips, roses, and peacocks were the chief decorative motifs used on this spatter ware which came from Staffordshire. It was a heavy white earthenware strong enough to withstand the ordinary vicissitudes of transportation over rough roads in Conestoga wagons. In the face of this English competition, many small Pennsylvania potteries which for a century had been turning out slip ware—America's first decorated pottery—closed down.

The blacksmiths, like the potters and other Pennsylvania craftsmen, favored the tulip as a decorative motif. Door latches were made with the cusps or flattened parts of the handle by which they are fastened to the door in the shape of tulips and hearts. Although people who buy old houses for restoration seldom give it a thought, it is an anachronism to use a Pennsylvania latch on a New England house. Yet in the days when the settlers did a good deal of moving about, they sometimes took their wrought-iron latches with them or had the blacksmith make new ones of the same design they were accustomed to in the place whence they came. In parts of Pennsylvania settled by New Englanders it would not be surprising to see old houses equipped with latches of the swordfish, bean, arrowhead, or ball-and-spear design. At least it would not be so startling as it was for me to see recently in Essex, Connecticut, a rose-red barn half as old as time with a Pennsylvania barn symbol or hex mark painted on it.

Incidentally, there is in Greenwich Village, New York, a shop where ceramic jewelry is made, including brooches designed and colored like Pennsylvania hex signs.

While door latches offered little chance for the smiths to exercise their decorative talents, the iron work on Conestoga wagons gave them a good opportunity to indulge their bent for design. The wrought-iron hinges and straps of the tool box midway of the wagon on the left side were beautifully designed, the sloping box lid presenting an excellent field for ornamental flourishes. This iron work was a distinctive feature of every Conestoga wagon. Many examples may be seen at the Landis Valley Museum near Lancaster.

The most notable artistic achievements of the Pennsylvania German ironmasters, however, were the cast-iron stove plates and fire-backs made at their charcoal furnaces, of which there were scores scattered through the Eastern counties. The relief designs for these stove plates were carved on wood blocks which were then impressed in sand to form the molds for casting the iron. Biblical scenes and conventional designs of tulips and hearts with familiar proverbs were used on jamb stoves. Adam and Eve, Elijah and the Ravens, and similar subjects were popular. Baron Stiegel cast some remarkable scenic stove plates at his Elizabeth furnace.

Iron plates with quaint sayings in the nature of house blessings or with the owner's name and building dates were made to be set into the exterior walls of houses. It was also an old Pennsylvania custom to place an iron Indian with bow and arrow on the doorway or roof of houses situated on land purchased from the Indians as a protection. One of these pieces of ironmongery is in the Metropolitan Museum, New York. Artistic locks were another product of the Pennsylvania German ironworkers.

The furniture of the Dutch country was of excellent workmanship and expressive of the people who liked it and bought it for their homes. It was solid and comely. Years ago, sophisticated collectors discovered this furniture and began looting farmhouses of their heirlooms, but there is still a good deal of it left among the descendants of the old families.

Plain and conservative in their own dress, the Pennsylvania Germans loved to surround themselves with colorfully decorated things. Their pine and poplar dower chests and bride boxes were magnificent in decorative design and color. Like their gorgeously woven coverlets, these chests were the work of specialists possessing extraordinary decorative skill, who circulated through the country. Certain counties seemed to favor certain designs. Berks County dower chests, for example, have a central panel in which a pair of heraldic unicorns, traditionally the protectors of maidenhood, confront each other. But no matter what the county, the ubiquitous tulip appears on practically all chests.

To the Pennsylvania German fondness for color we owe the custom of dyeing eggs at Easter. This tradition they brought from the Old World. From Eastern Pennsylvania it spread to other colonies and it is now a universal American custom. These folk also introduced the Easter rabbit.

Another quaint custom is that of the Christmas

putz, or Nativity scene, with miniature figures of carved and painted wood representing the Christ Child, Mary, Joseph, the Shepherds and Wise Men, with cattle, sheep, and other animals standing about. Great pains are taken in the construction and decoration of these home-made models, which may be simple or elaborate and arranged in any way the maker pleases. The only condition is that the *putz* must have for its central theme the story of the Nativity. If it doesn't, it isn't a *putz*.

The custom of building these Christmas scenes was brought to this country by the Moravians in the days when New Englanders ignored Christmas. Although the custom prevails throughout the Dutch country, the *putz* has been most popular in the places that were settled by the Moravians—Bethlehem, Nazareth, Reading, Oley, Allentown, Emmaus, Hebron, and Lititz. Between Christmas and Twelfth Night the Moravians in Bethlehem used to go *putzing* to see the cribs or créches their neighbors had created and everywhere were treated to wine and the special Moravian Christmas cookies. It was a season of open house and even strangers were welcome, but so many outsiders came to see the cribs that finally, in self-defence, the Moravians had to shut them out. But the *putz* still prevails as a feature of the Christmas celebration and has spread to other communities outside the state.

There is, of course, no greater name in the history of American glass than that of Heinrich Wilhelm Stiegel, who came to America with a party of immigrants in 1750 and a dozen years later began the manufacture of glassware at Manheim in Lancaster County. With the aid of glassworkers whom he imported from various parts of Europe, Stiegel produced the first flint glass for tableware in the colonies. It was the most beautiful glass made in America, unsurpassed by even the finest European glass. Pure and even in color, it was made in a variety of colors, including clear white, blue, green, amethyst, amber, and opaque white. Stiegel himself seems to have been fondest of blue, for this color dominated the output of the Manheim works. Engraving or enameling in color enhanced the beauty of many of his pieces. Stiegel did not make his glass for any luxury market but for the common trade.

Many stories are told of this great artist whose grand manners and extravagant mode of living won him the courtesy title of Baron Stiegel. He used to ride in a coach drawn by six white horses and give great parties at his "castles." His activities as a glass manufacturer continued for only about a dozen years, but they are the most important years in the history of the American glass industry. In 1774 the baron lost his business, suffered imprisonment for debt, and never succeeded in recouping his fallen fortunes. The great value placed on Stiegel glass today is not so much on account of its age and rarity as because of its superb quality and absolute beauty of design.

IT IS not surprising that piety for the past should be a Pennsylvania trait and the upholding of tradition one of the customs of the commonwealth. Pennsylvania was in more than the geographical sense the keystone of the colonies. Historically, it is as notable a piece of territory as there is in the United States. It is fortunate, therefore, that, during periods of change in which traditions are apt to crumble, it has retained its acute awareness of the past and remained faithful to those traditions.

Happily, too, Pennsylvania historians have not been so preoccupied with the main events and movements of history as to overlook those purely parochial trifles and straws that are often more revealing of the character, temperament, environment, and achievements of the people than the full-dress ceremonies of history. Sherman Day, for example, in his *Pennsylvania Historical Collections*, published in 1843, laid up a rich harvest of regional anecdotes of which the following, with the exception of one or two taken from other sources, are typical. They were mostly garnered by him from newspapers, personal reminiscences, and local histories, and all are more than a century old. In saving them from oblivion, Day was observing the old Pennsylvania custom of looking backward.

"Madam,—I have written to Mr.—, of your city, an account of an affair between a white man and two Indians. I am now about to give you a relation in which you will see how a person of your sex acquitted herself in defence of her own life and that of her husband and children.

"The lady who is the subject of this story, is named Experience Bozarth. She lives on a creek called Dunkard Creek, in the southwest corner of this county. About the middle of March last, two or three families, who were afraid to stay at home, gathered to her house and there stayed—looking on themselves to be safer than when all scattered about at their own houses.

"On a certain day, some of the children thus collected came running in from play, in great haste, saying, there were ugly redmen. One of the men in the house stepped to the door, where he received a ball in the side of his breast, which caused him to fall back into the house. The Indian was immediately in over him, and engaged with another man who was in the house. The man tossed the Indian on a bed, and called for a knife to kill him. (Observe, these were all the men that were in the house.) Now Mrs. Bozarth appears the only help, who not finding a knife at hand, took up an axe that lay by, and with one blow cut out the brains of the Indian. At that instant, (for all was instantaneous,) a second Indian entered the door, and shot the man dead, who was engaged with the Indian on the bed. Mrs. Bozarth turned to this second Indian, and with her axe gave him several large cuts, some of which let his entrails appear. He bawled out, murder. On this, sundry other Indians, (who had hitherto been fully employed, killing some children out of doors,) came rushing to his relief; the head of one of these Mrs. Bozarth clave in two with her axe, as he stuck it in at the door, which laid him flat upon the ground. Another snatched hold of the wounded, bellowing fellow, and pulled him out of doors; and Mrs. Bozarth, with the assistance of the man who was first shot in the door, and by this time a little recovered, shut the door after them, and fastened it, where they kept garrison for several days, the dead white man and dead Indian both in the house with them, and the Indians about the house besieging them. At length they were relieved by a party sent for that purpose. This whole affair, to shutting the door, was not, perhaps, more than three minutes in acting.

"Westmoreland, April 26, 1779."

"Chief Justice M'Kean resided here [Harrisburg] for some time, at least while Congress sat at York. He lived in a substantial one-story log house, a short space above what is now Locust Street. He wore an immense cocked hat, and had great deference shown him by the country people, and the Indians who had their village on what is now M'Kee's place. This was in 1778-79; after the country was quieted, when he and the other judges of the Supreme Court came to Harrisburg to hold court, numbers of citizens of the place would go out on horseback to meet them and escort them into town. Sometimes one or two hundred people would attend for the purpose. The sheriff with his rod of office, and other public officers, and the bar, would attend on the occasion; and each morning whilst the Chief Justice was in town, holding court, the sheriff and constables escorted him from his lodgings to the court room. The Chief Justice, when on the bench, sat with his hat on, and was dressed in a scarlet gown."

"Allegheny College originated in the public spirit of a number of intelligent citizens of Meadville, at a meeting held 20th June, 1815. Rev. Timothy Alden was appointed President, and Professor of Languages and Ecclesiastical History, and Rev. Robert Johnson, Vice-President, and Professor of Moral Science. The institution was opened the 4th of July, 1816. Rev. Mr. Alden was inaugurated amid an astonishing display of dead languages. The very valuable library which the institution possesses, was obtained mainly by the untiring zeal of Mr. Alden, who performed one or more tours through the eastern states to solicit aid from learned and benevolent individuals for his infant seminary. The most liberal contributor was the Rev. Dr. Bentley, a Unitarian clergyman, of Salem, Mass., who had spent his life in amassing one of the most rare collections of theological works in the country. Harvard University had set her eye upon this collection, and having bestowed the preliminary plum, in the shape of an LL.D. diploma, patiently awaited the doctor's demise. She occupied, however, the situation of Esau before Isaac, for Mr. Alden had previously prepared the savory dish, and received the boon; and the name of Bentley Hall now records the gratitude of Allegheny College."

"1732. A violent contest for member of the Assembly took place between Andrew Galbraith and John Wright. Mrs. Galbraith rode through the town at the head of a numerous band of horsemen, friends of her husband. In consequence of her activity, her husband was elected [from Lancaster County]."

"There was another fort in Sinking Valley, at the lead-mine; and William Moore, finding it necessary to go there for ammunition, started very early one morning, with a boy by the name of M'Cartney. As he was passing a log by the side of the road, with some brush behind it, a shot from an Indian in ambush caused him to jump several feet into the air; and he started off into the bushes, in a direction opposite to that which he should naturally have taken— his brain being undoubtedly bewildered by the shot. The boy and the Indian at once jumped behind trees; but the latter peeping out from his tree, which was not large, the boy availed himself of the chance to put a bullet into his buttock, which was exposed at the other side. The Indian ran, and dropped his belt and knife; and the road was found strewed with bunches of bloody leaves, with which he had attempted to stanch the wound. But the man himself was not found, though bones were afterwards found, supposed to be his."

"Among the eminent teachers in Philadelphia about the middle of the last century [the eighteenth] were Robert Proud, the historian, who was a Scotchman by birth; and David James Dove, an Englishman, much celebrated as a teacher, and no less as a small politician and a dealer in the minor kind of satirical poetry. Graydon relates the following anecdote of him: 'Dove was a humorist, and a person not unlikely to be engaged in ludicrous scenes. It was his practice, in his school, to substitute disgrace for corporal punishment. He had a contrivance for boys who were late in their morning attendance. This was to dispatch a committee of five or six scholars for them, with a bell and lighted lantern, and in this "odd equipage," in broad daylight, the bell all the while tingling, were they escorted through the streets to school. As Dove affected a strict regard for justice in his dispensations of punishment, and always professed willingness to have an equal measure of it meted out to himself in case of his transgressing, the boys took him at his word; and one morning, when he had overstaid his time, either through laziness, inattention, or design, he found himself waited on in the usual form. He immediately admitted the justice of the procedure, and, putting himself behind the lantern and bell, marched with great solemnity to school, to the no small gratification of the boys, and entertainment of the spectators.' "

"The acquisition of the indispensable articles of salt, iron, steel, and castings, presented great difficulties to the first settlers of the western country. They had no stores of any kind—no salt, iron, nor iron works; nor had they money to make purchases where those articles could be obtained. Peltry and furs were their only resources before they had time to raise cattle and horses for sale in the Atlantic states.

"Every family collected what peltry and fur they could obtain throughout the year, for the purpose of sending them over the mountains for barter. In the fall of the year, after seeding time, every family formed an association with some of their neighbors for starting the little caravan. A master-driver was selected from among them, who was to be assisted by one or more young men and sometimes a boy or two. The horses were fitted out with pack-saddles, to the hinder part of which was fastened a pair of hobbles made of hickory withes. A bell and collar ornamented their necks. The bags provided for the conveyance of the salt were filled with feed for the horses. On the journey, a part of this feed was left at convenient stages on the way down, to support the return of the caravan. Large wallets, well filled with bread, jirk, boiled ham, and cheese, furnished provision for the drivers. At night, after feeding, the horses (whether put in pasture or turned out into the woods) were hobbled, and the bells were opened.

"The barter for salt and iron was first made at Baltimore. Frederick, Hagerstown, Oldtown, and Fort Cumberland, in succession became the place of exchange. Each horse carried two bushels of alum salt, weighing 84 pounds the bushel. This, to be sure, was not a heavy load for the horses; but it was enough, considering the scanty subsistence allowed them on the journey. The common price of a bushel of alum salt, at an early period, was a cow and a calf; and, until weights were introduced, the salt was measured into the half-bushel by hand, as lightly as possible. No one was permitted to walk heavily over the floor while the operation of measuring was going on.

"The following anecdote will serve to show how little the native sons of the forest knew of the etiquette of the Atlantic cities:

"A neighbor of my father, some years after the

settlement of the country, had collected a small drove of cattle for the Baltimore market. Among the hands employed to drive them was one who never had seen any condition of society but that of woodsmen. At one of their lodging-places in the mountain, the landlord and his hired man, in the course of the night, stole two of the bells belonging to the drove, and hid them in a piece of woods. The drove had not gone far in the morning, before the bells were missed; and a detachment went back to recover them. The men were found reaping in the field of the landlord. They were accused of the theft, but they denied the charge. The torture of sweating according to the custom of that time—that is, of suspension by the arms pinioned behind their backs —brought a confession. The bells were procured, and hung around the necks of the thieves. In this condition they were driven on foot before the detachment, until they overtook the drove, which by this time had gone nine miles. A halt was called and a jury selected to try the culprits. They were condemned to receive a certain number of lashes on the bare back from the hand of each drover. The man above alluded to was the owner of one of the bells. When it came to his turn to use the hickory, 'Now, (says he to the thief,) you infernal scoundrel, I'll work your jacket nineteen to the dozen. Only think what a rascally figure I should make in the

streets of Baltimore, without a bell on my horse!'
The man was in earnest. Having seen no horses used
without bells, he thought they were requisite in
every situation."

At the battle and massacre of Wyoming in 1778,
seven men went out to fight from the farm of Mr.
Weeks, five sons and sons-in-law and two inmates.
"Not one escaped, the whole seven fell, and the old
man was left like the oak struck by lightning—withered, bare, blasted—all its boughs torn away. The
battle was on Friday. On Sunday morning twenty
Indians came to his house and ordered breakfast.
They told Mr. Weeks he must go—he could not stay
—he must clear out. 'All my sons have fallen,' said
the old man, 'and here I am left with fourteen
grandchildren, all young and helpless.' After breakfast, one of the Indian leaders stepped up to Mr.
Weeks, took the hat from his head, and put it on;
he then wheeled into the middle of the street a large
rocking chair with a cushion in it, sat himself down,
and rocked himself. The tigers, gorged with food,
blood, and plunder, for the moment paused, and
rocked themselves into something like good nature.
In sending the family into exile, they allowed them
a pair of oxen and a wagon to carry the children, a
bed and some food. They went up the Lackawanna
to Orange County, New York."

"We had in those days [at Philadelphia during the Revolution] a newspaper published by Charles Town once a week, called the *Evening Post*,—which Jimmy McCoy, an Irishman with one leg, used to sell through the streets—blowing a trumpet, and crying out, 'Here's your bloody news! Here's your fine bloody news!' "

"About the year 1793, a fever of a violent character prevailed here [Harrisburg], especially among the new settlers or foreigners. At the same time, the yellow fever was prevailing in Philadelphia, and fears were entertained of its introduction into Harrisburg. A patrol was accordingly established at the lower end of town, to prevent infected persons from Philadelphia coming into it. A considerable number of Irish emigrants died, and some of the citizens; but most families of the place were to some extent afflicted. A mill-dam owned by two men named Landis, was generally thought to be the cause of this sickness. The citizens, after various meetings, resolved (in March, 1795) on its removal; and a subscription was set on foot to raise money to pay the Landises for the property. The site of the mill-dam, and race, had been bought from John Harris. The money raised was tendered to the Landises, who refused it. The citizens then prepared for the forcible removal of the dam, and the Landises

[233]

threatened to use force to prevent it. The citizens accordingly marched in a body to the dam, on a cold snowy day in March. The owners were there, with several men, armed with guns, threatening to fire. The citizens, however, advanced into the water, and the dam was soon demolished. The Landises threatened a suit, and the citizens handed to them a list of several hundred names to be sued; but the proprietors finally took the money.

"It may be remarked that some citizens of Harrisburg, who refused to contribute to the subscription, were obliged to leave the place. No violence was offered them, but no one would employ them in their pursuits, and they at length went elsewhere."

"There had long existed a tradition in this region that Braddock was killed by one of his own men, and more recent developments leave little or no doubt of the fact. A recent writer in the *National Intelligencer*, whose authority is good on such points, says:

" 'When my father was removing with his family to the west, one of the Fausetts kept a public house to the eastward from, and near where Uniontown now stands, as the county seat of Fayette, Pennsylvania. This man's house we lodged in about the tenth of October, 1781, twenty-six years and a few months after Braddock's defeat, and there it was made anything but a secret that one of the family dealt the death-blow to the British general.

" 'Thirteen years afterwards I met Thomas Fausett in Fayette County, then, as he told me, in his 70th year. To him I put the plain question, and received the plain reply, "I did shoot him!" He then went on to insist, that, by doing so, he contributed to save what was left of the army. In brief, in my youth I never heard the fact either doubted or blamed, that Fausett shot Braddock.'

"Hon. Andrew Stewart of Uniontown, says he knew and often conversed with Tom Fausett, who did not hesitate to avow in the presence of his friends that he shot General Braddock. Fausett was a man of gigantic frame, of uncivilized half-savage propensities, and spent most of his life among the mountains as a hermit, living on the game which he killed. He would occasionally come into town and get drunk. Sometimes he would repel inquiries into the affair of Braddock's death by putting his fingers to his lips, and uttering a sort of buzzing sound; at others he would burst into tears, and appear greatly agitated by conflicting passions.

"In spite of Braddock's silly order that the troops should not protect themselves behind the trees, Joseph Fausett had taken such position, when Braddock rode up in a passion, and struck him down with his sword. Tom Fausett, who was but a short distance from his brother, saw the whole transaction, and immediately drew up his rifle and shot Braddock through the lungs, partly in revenge for the outrage upon his brother, and partly, as he always alleged, to get the general out of the way, and thus save the remainder of the gallant band who had been sacrificed to his obstinacy and want of experience in frontier warfare."

"The impulse given to the lumber-trade, by the speculations in the state of Maine, was not without its influence upon remote sections of the Union. The keen sagacity of the Yankees discovered that there were vast bodies of pine-lands lying around the sources of the Allegheny River, not appreciated at their full value by the few pioneers who lived among them. The Yankees had learned to estimate the value of pine-land by the tree and by the log: the Pennsylvanians still reckoned it by the acre. Somewhere between 1830 and 1837, individuals and companies from New England and New York purchased considerable bodies of land on the head-waters of Red Bank and Clarion Rivers, from the Holland Land Co., and other large landholders. They proceeded to erect saw-mills, and to drive the lumber-trade after the most approved method. The little leaven thus introduced caused quite a fermentation among the lumbermen and landholders of the county. More lands changed owners; new water privileges were improved; capital was introduced from abroad; and during the spring floods every creek and river resounded with the preparation of rafts, and the lively shouts of the lumbermen as they shot their rafts over the swift chutes of the mill-dams."

"The business of Warren varies with the season of the year. In the midst of winter or summer the place is exceedingly dull; but at the breaking up of the ice in the spring, and during the subsequent floods, the town and the whole country above, on the Conewango and Allegheny, is alive with the bustle of preparation among the lumbermen. Large rafts are continually coming down the Allegheny, and smaller ones down the Conewango, and rounding in at Warren to be coupled into rafts of immense area, 60 or 70 feet wide, and from 250 to 300 feet long, in which shape they pursue their course to Pittsburgh and Cincinnati. Large boats, too, or 'broad horns,' as they are called, from the width of their oars, form part of the fleet.

"The rafts, like immense floating islands, form at once a vehicle and the temporary residence of several families on their way down the river. Old and young, from the gray-haired pioneer of sixty down to the boy of twelve years, are interested in their departure, and compose the crews to navigate them. There is probably not a boy of twelve years old living on any stream in Warren County who has not made his voyage to Cincinnati, perhaps to 'Orleans.'

"It is a cheering sight to see the bright broad raft floating slowly down the picturesque passes of the Allegheny, with its little shanties, and busy population; some lifting the long heavy oars, some cooking at the great fire, some eating their bacon from a broad clean shingle—superior to French porcelain —some lounging in the sun, and some practising with their coarse wit upon the gazers from the shore, and making the wild hills echo with their shouts."

"The mining population of our coal regions is almost exclusively composed of foreigners, principally from England and Wales, with a few Irish and Scotchmen. The former have a decided preference for working in small veins, and they can use the pick in the narrowest space, right and left, and in all positions. They cannot, of course, swing it over their shoulders, or give it the force which is deemed so necessary for effective work; but holding it in front, and making short, quick strokes, the pick is still as effective in their hands, in a space of three or four feet, (or even less) as would be in less circumscribed limits.

"This predilection of the English miners is principally attributable to the fact, that the coal veins of their mining regions are usually thin, and having entered them at a very early age, they have thus formed a preference for thin veins, and a prejudice against large ones, where it is necessary to blast, use ladders, etc. Every miner carries his lamp on his cap, to which it is hooked. While pursuing their labors in the mines, they soon become thoroughly covered over with the black coal dust, and their clothes, which are of the coarsest fabrics, rudely patched together, are saturated with water. The mines are damp, and the floor usually full of coal-mud and water; hence the miners and laborers wear heavy coarse shoes, with the soles covered with tacks. Although extremely healthy as a class, they are nevertheless pale and somewhat delicate in the face, and their eyes may be said to be prominent. Their features are not regular, and they cannot justly lay claim to manly beauty. They know little but what pertains to their subterraneous employments; making that the subject of their discussions, their jests and their pastimes, they have little care for things concerning the upper crust. They are, to a certain degree, superstitious; even the most intelligent of them yield to it. For example, it is considered an evil omen when a stranger, in entering the mine, begins to whistle. It produces a certain effect among them and destroys, in a measure, their good spirits.

A miner never whistles, and when, occasionally, they hum a tune, it is more of a soft and plaintive character than the popular songs of the day. The employment seems well calculated to indulge thought —calm, complacent ideas. There is no wildness, no ambition; they seek only contentment, and are satisfied with their lot."

"Philadelphia, 17th Feb. 1842. This morning, at about 6 o'clock, Mr. J. G. Boyd, late cashier and agent of the Towanda Bank, killed himself, at his residence in Schuylkill Seventh St., by firing a loaded pistol into his mouth. Previously to his late dismissal as the cashier of the bank, it was ascertained that he had, as the signing officer of the relief issues of that bank, put out some thousands of dollars on his own account. The Penn Township Bank, one of the losers by this fraudulent issue, and by some of his other transactions, had commenced a suit against him and it was while in the custody of the sheriff, and when he saw that the whole fraud must be exposed, that he committed the melancholy act. About two years since he had married an interesting young lady at Trenton, New Jersey, and was keeping house with her at the time of his suicide in Philadelphia. He had furnished this house splendidly—had settled upon his wife a farm near Germantown, worth about $8,000, and had made many munificent presents to her relatives. But it appears that all this time he had another wife, a most estimable lady, at Covington, Tioga County, by whom he had several children, and with whom he was living on most affectionate terms, whenever his business called him to that vicinity. With his Philadelphia wife he passed as Mr. Henry Seymour—represented himself as a drover having large transactions with the interior counties, and often spoke of his intimate friend Mr. John G. Boyd. So adroitly was the deception maintained, that neither of these unfortunate ladies ever suspected the least impropriety in his conduct, or alienation of his affections."

"A most singular incident recently occurred at the table of one of our most respected farmers (Mr. Ruch), in this neighborhood. The family had baked some pies early in the morning, and had set them in the cellar to cool for dinner. It was observed, before the pie was cut, that it appeared very full; and no sooner was the knife thrust into it, than a snake issued out, to the utter amazement and terror of all at the table. This was a kind of dessert as unwelcome as unexpected. The snake, it was supposed, had got in between the crusts while the pie was cooling on the cellar floor."—*Sunbury American.*

"A young lady suddenly appeared at a lonely cabin, almost in a state of nudity, in great distress from cold and hunger, and her limbs and wrists galled and bloody, as if they had been chafed with a rope. For some time she could scarcely speak. At length she recovered strength enough to say that she had been travelling on horseback, from her uncle's in Kentucky, where she had been at school, to Montreal, where her parents resided. She had been accompanied by one Benjamin Connet, a Canadian, either an agent or servant of her father, whom he had sent expressly to conduct her home. Not far from the cabin, in a lonely part of the road, he had presented a pistol at her, compelled her to dismount, stripped her, robbed her of all her money as well as her clothing, tied her to a tree, and left her there to perish with hunger, or be devoured by wild beasts. She had remained in that situation all night, when, after the most desperate struggles, she had extricated herself. After being refreshed, she went with the family and pointed out the tree, and the path she had beaten round it in her struggles to get loose. There was something artless in her appearance; and her modest demeanor, and delicate frame, left no doubt in the minds of those who saw her that her statement was true. She appeared to be over-·whelmed with distress at the thought of her situation. Her name she said was Esther McDowell. The kind people of the cabin soothed her distress, clothed her, and took her on as far as Williamsport, where she was lodged with a worthy and pious family, until news could be conveyed to Montreal.

"In the mean time, public indignation was highly excited against the villain Connet; the chivalry of the West Branch was aroused, and scouts and hand-bills were sent out in all directions. He had twenty-four hours' start, however, and had eluded all observation; for no one had seen any stranger pass, answering his description. Two or three weeks had elapsed, and no news was heard of the villain: no letters had been received from Montreal; nor had any discoveries been made concerning this mysterious affair, except that a bundle of man's clothes had been found hidden near where the robbery was committed. These might have been left by the robber, who had shifted his suit. Some people were malicious enough to insinuate that the young lady had robbed herself; but her deportment in the family where she lodged was a triumphant answer to any such base insinuations. She was lady-like in her manners, highly intelligent, and possessing a well-cultivated mind; and if not pious, at any rate piously disposed. She rather modestly avoided, than sought society, and would only converse with persons of the most sedate character. Time, however, wore away; no news was received from Montreal; and the number of the suspicious began to increase. The clothing found near the tree had been recognised as that of a young tailor, who had lived for some time in a neighboring town, and had lately moved away. Some of those who knew the tailor happened to visit Miss McDowell, and there, forsooth, they found the very face, which the young tailor had worn, upon her shoulders. Here was a development! Since the secret was out, she confessed that she was the daughter of highly respectable Quaker parents in Philadelphia: she had been beguiled into evil ways; but detesting the career of vice, she fled from the city, and, trusting to her needle for support, she had, with no less ingenuity than enterprise, established herself as a gentleman tailor, in one of the villages on the West Branch. She succeeded tolerably well in her new sex and profession; but eventually becoming tired of it, she adopted the stratagem described above. Her duped, but still sympathizing friends, restored her to her disconsolate parents; and it was learned afterwards that she went to the west, under a new name, and was married. The whole affair was some months in progress, before its final development; and after it was out, many a wise one chuckled, as he said to his neighbor, 'I t-o-l-d you so!' "

"I am ruralizing for a week in a fertile vale of deep-soiled red shale, underlying the lime-stone of the Moxatawney valley. The peasantry are honest, hard-working Germans. Here they lock no doors.

The congregations, of different sectarian faith, worship in the same church on alternate Sundays. The
church is filled with attentive people, and a very
great proportion are communicants. They have an
excellent organ, made in this county. Preaching in
German. It pains me to observe in every country
churchyard the naked marble slabs, unsheltered by
a single tree, and unadorned by a single shrub or
flower.

"A contented mind is generally associated with
the life of a farmer, by our novelists at least, and by
those who get their notions from such sources. But
farming is far from being exempt from the petty
vexations that constitute the stinging annoyances of
life; and it is an undoubted fact, that the worship of
the dollar finds among this class the most devout
adherents. My companion pointed to a house near
Kutztown, where, a few weeks since, a farmer in
good circumstances hung himself, because he had
$200 of the notes of a bank that had stopped pay-
ment; and many years ago, I remember a wealthy
farmer in the same valley, who destroyed himself
in the same way, because he had on hand in the
spring all of his wheat, and could not sell it at the
price he was offered during the winter."

"The 8th of January, 1841, will be long remembered on the Delaware for one of the highest and

most destructive floods ever known along the river. Houses, barns, fences, furniture, haystacks, coal boats, saw logs, bridges and cakes of ice, were borne by the destructive tide. Not a bridge was left standing between Easton and Trenton, nor on the Lehigh between Easton and Mauch Chunk.

"Center bridge came floating down in two massive pieces just before noon. One piece struck New Hope bridge about midway, with an awful crash, carrying away one arch on the Jersey side. The Jersey pier soon gave way, when the third arch followed, and lodged a short distance below. The other part on the Pennsylvania side remained. George B. Fell, who happened to be on Center bridge, was carried away with it. Fearing danger from the crushing of its timbers over head, he succeeded in reaching, with the aid of a plank, a broken portion of the roof floating near him, thus freeing himself from the main structure. When he passed New Hope bridge he was upon a loose plank, and was obliged to lie flat upon it to avoid touching the bridge. Attempts were made in vain to rescue him at that and various other places. At Yardleyville he struck a pier, and got splashed with water. When he had passed under the bridge and floated a few yards below, the whole structure was precipitated into the stream. He continued to float, gathering pieces of lumber, which he kept together, forming a sort of raft, by which he was enabled to steer into the still water about three miles above Trenton, where he was taken up in safety. On his return to Lambertville, he was received with shouts and the discharge of a cannon."

After the battle of Trenton, December 26, 1776, the Hessian prisoners were paraded through the streets of Philadelphia. Here is what a Hessian corporal wrote of this experience.

"Big and little, old and young, stood there to see what sort of mortals we might be. When we came directly in front of them they looked sharply at us. The old women howled dreadfully, and wanted to throttle us all, because we had come to America to rob them of their freedom. Some others, in spite of all the scolding, brought brandy and bread, and wanted to give them to us, but the old women would not allow it, and still wished to strangle us. The American guard that had us in charge had received orders from Washington to lead us all about the town, so that everybody should see us; but the people crowded in on us with great fury, and nearly overpowered the guard. So when we were near the barracks our commanding officer said: 'Dear Hessians, let us march into these barracks.' We did so, and the whole American detachment had to check the raging people."

"The furniture for the table, for several years after the settlement of this country, consisted of a few pewter dishes, plates, and spoons; but mostly of wooden bowls, trenchers, and noggins. If these last were scarce, gourds and hard-shelled squashes made up the deficiency. The iron pots, knives, and forks, were brought from the east side of the mountains, along with the salt and iron, on packhorses.

"These articles of furniture corresponded very well with the articles of diet on which they were employed. 'Hog and hominy' were proverbial for the dish of which they were the component parts. Jonny cake and pone were, at the outset of the settlements of the country, the only forms of bread in use for breakfast and dinner. At supper, milk and mush were the standard dish.

"In our whole display of furniture, the delft, china, and silver were unknown. It did not then, as now, require contributions from the four quarters of the globe to furnish the breakfast table—yet our homely fare, and unsightly cabins, and furniture, produced a hardy veteran race, who planted the first footsteps of society and civilization in the immense regions of the west.

"I well recollect the first time I ever saw a teacup and saucer, and tasted coffee. My mother died when I was about six or seven years of age. My father then

sent me to Maryland with a brother of my grandfather, Mr. Alexander Wells, to school.

"At Col. Brown's in the mountains, at Stoney
Creek glades, I for the first time saw tame geese; and
by bantering a pet gander, I got a severe biting by
his bill and beating by his wings. I wondered very
much that birds so large and strong should be so
much tamer than the wild turkeys; at this place,
however, all was right, excepting the large birds
which they called geese. The cabin and its furniture
were such as I had been accustomed to see in the
backwoods, as my country was then called.

"At Bedford everything was changed. The tavern
at which my uncle put up was a stone house, and to
make the change still more complete, it was plas-
tered on the inside, both as to the walls and ceiling.
On going into the dining room, I was struck with
astonishment at the appearance of the house. I had
no idea that there was any house in the world which
was not built of logs; but here I looked round the
house and could see no logs, and above I could see no
joists. Whether such a thing had been made by the
hands of man, or had grown so of itself, I could not
conjecture. I had not the courage to inquire anything about it. When supper came on, my confusion
was worse confounded. A little cup stood in a bigger
one with some brownish looking stuff in it, which
was neither milk, hominy, nor broth: what to do

with these little cups, and the little spoon belonging to them, I could not tell; and I was afraid to ask anything concerning the use of them.

"I therefore watched attentively to see what the big folks would do with their little cups and spoons. I imitated them, and found the taste of the coffee nauseous beyond anything I ever had tasted in my life. I continued to drink, as the rest of the company did, with the tears streaming from my eyes; but when it was to end I was at a loss to know, as the little cups were filled immediately after being emptied. This circumstance distressed me very much, as I durst not say I had enough. Looking attentively at the grown persons, I saw one man turn his little cup bottom upwards and put his little spoon across it. I observed that after this his cup was not filled again. I followed his example, and to my great satisfaction, the result as to my cup was the same.

"The introduction of delft ware, was considered by many of the backwoods people as a culpable innovation. It was too easily broken, and the plates of that ware dulled their scalping and clasp knives. Tea ware was too small for men;—it might do for women and children. Tea and coffee were only slops which, in the adage of the day, 'did not stick by the ribs.' The idea was, they were designed only for people of quality, who do not labor, or the sick. A genuine

backwoodsman would have thought himself dis-
graced by showing a fondness for those slops."

"The king's proclamation was set up in various
places, prohibiting any person from trading with
the Indians until further orders. Notwithstanding
all this, about the 1st of March, 1765, a number of
wagons, loaded with Indian goods and warlike
stores, were sent from Philadelphia to Henry Pol-
lens, Conococheague; and from thence seventy pack-
horses were loaded with these goods, in order to
carry them to Fort Pitt. This alarmed the country,
and Mr. William Duffield raised about fifty armed
men, and met the pack-horses at the place where
Mercersburg now stands. Mr. Duffield desired the
employers to store up their goods and not proceed
until further orders. They made light of this, and
went over the North Mountain, where they lodged
in a small valley called the Great Cove. Mr. Duffield
and his party followed after, and came to their lodging, and again urged them to store up their goods.
He reasoned with them on the impropriety of their
proceedings, and what the frontier inhabitants
would be exposed to if the Indians should now get a
supply; he said, as it was well known that they had
scarcely any ammunition, and were almost naked,
to supply them now would be a kind of murder, and
would be illegally trading at the expense of the blood

and treasure of the frontiers. Notwithstanding his powerful reasoning, these traders made game of what he said, and would only answer him by ludicrous burlesque.

"When I beheld this, and found that Mr. Duffield would not compel them to store up their goods, I collected ten of my old warriors, that I had formerly disciplined in the Indian way, went off privately after night, and encamped in the woods. The next day, as usual, we blacked and painted, and waylaid them near Sidelong Hill. I scattered my men about forty rods along the side of the road, and ordered every two to take a tree, and about eight or ten rods between each couple, with orders to keep a reserved fire—one not to fire until his comrade had loaded his gun: by this means we kept up a constant slow fire upon them, from front to rear. We then heard nothing of these traders' merriment or burlesque. When they saw their pack-horses falling close by them, they called out, 'Pray, gentlemen, what would you have us to do?' The reply was, 'Collect all your loads to the front, and unload them in one place; take your private property, and immediately retire.' When they were gone, we burnt what they left, which consisted of blankets, shirts, vermilion, lead, beads, wampum, tomahawks, scalping-knives, etc."

"Stephen Girard was born of very humble parents, near Bordeaux in France, on the 24th of May, 1750. Such education as he ever had, he must have picked up in the world at large. He commenced his career at the age of ten or twelve—leaving France for the first and last time, as a cabin boy, bound to the West Indies. Thence he went to New York, and sailed for some years between there and the West Indies and New Orleans, as cabin-boy, sailor, mate, and eventually master and owner. Having made some money, he started a small shop in Water Street, Philadelphia, in 1769, and in 1770 married a pretty girl, the daughter of a caulker. He lived with her some twenty years; but not very happily, on account of his own asperity of temper. She became insane in 1790, and died in the Philadelphia Hospital in 1815. An only child died in infancy. After his marriage he continued business in Water Street, occasionally going as master of his own vessels—in one of which he was captured on a voyage to St. Domingo. He came home poor, and started a little cider and wine bottling shop in Water Street, aided by his wife, the year before the Revolutionary War. He was a friend to the Revolution, and removed to Mount Holly while the British occupied Philadelphia. About the year 1782 he took on lease a number of stores on Water Street, which proved a profitable operation, —and afterwards went into business with his brother, Captain John Girard, who came out from

France. They drove a profitable trade with St. Domingo; and at their dissolution (for they could not agree) John was worth $60,000, and Stephen $30,000. After this he went largely into the St. Domingo trade; and while a brig and schooner of his were lying at Cape Françoise, the great revolt of the Negroes occurred. Many planters, in the panic, removed their valuables on board his vessels and again returning to the shore, were cut off by the Negroes. Whole families thus perished together; and Mr. Girard, by the most extensive advertising, could never ascertain the heirs of the wealth (said to be about $50,000) that thus fell into his hands. His next commercial enterprises were in the East India trade, in which he had several ships, and acquired a large fortune. At the expiration of the charter of the old United States Bank in 1810-11, he purchased, through the Barings, in London, about $500,000 of that stock; and not long afterwards—purchasing the banking-house of the institution in Third Street, and making an arrangement with the former cashier, Mr. George Simpson—he started his own private bank in May, 1812, with a capital of $1,200,000. This was a bold step at the opening of the war with Great Britain—yet the specie was never refused for a bank-note of Stephen Girard's. When the new United States Bank was started, in 1816, he waited until the last moment before the subscription books closed, and then, inquiring if all that wished had subscribed, he coolly took the balance of the stock, amounting to $3,100,000; some of which he afterwards parted with. By the subsequent rise of this stock his fortune was immensely augmented. His own bank was continued till his death, when it had accumulated a capital of $4,000,000. The bank was afterwards chartered by the legislature as the Girard Bank, with individual stockholders; and has since failed. Mr. Girard died of influenza, on the 26th of December 1831, at his residence in Water, above Market Street.

"Stephen Girard was exceedingly plain in his dress and personal appearance. He was always blind of one eye; and in middle life might be mistaken for a stout sailor, and in maturer years for a plain old farmer. His dwelling-house was under the same roof with his counting-house, in Water Street—a neighborhood occupied entirely by stores; and his furniture was of the plainest kind. His equipage was an old chaise and a plain farm-horse. He indulged in no pleasures, or scenes of social life; had no one with whom he sympathized as a friend; and when his sympathies were exercised at all, they seemed to be for masses of men, and not for individuals—for future generations, and not for the present. He had a sort of instinctive fondness for giving medical advice; and when the yellow-fever desolated the city, in 1793, regardless of danger, he spent his whole time in personal attendance upon the sick, in all parts of the city. His temper was irritable, and when excited he would break out upon his dependents, in his broken English, with great volubility."

"A more intelligent, virtuous, and resolute class of men never settled any country, than the first settlers of Western Pennsylvania; and the women who shared their sufferings and sacrifices were no less worthy. Very many of the settlers in what are now Washington and Allegheny counties were professors of religion of the strictest sect of Seceders. At a very early period, a distinguished minister of that denomination, Mr. Henderson, was settled near Canonsburgh. It was common for families to ride from ten to fifteen miles to meeting. The young people regularly walked five or six miles, and in summer carried their stockings and shoes, if they had any, in their hands. I furnished the audience with seats. Among the men who attended public worship in winter, ten were obliged to substitute a blanket or coverlet for a great coat, where one enjoyed the luxury of that article. So great was the destitution of comfortable clothing, that when the first court of Common Pleas was held in Catfish, now Washington, a highly respectable citizen, whose presence was required as a magistrate, could not attend court without first borrowing a pair of leather breeches from an equally respectable neighbor who was summoned on the grand jury. The latter lent them, and having no others, had to stay at home. This scarcity of clothing will not seem surprising when we consider the condition of the country at that time, and that most of these settlers brought but a scanty supply of clothing and bedding with them. Their stock could not be replenished until flax was grown and made into cloth.

"The labor of all the settlers was greatly interrupted by the Indian war. Although the older settlers had some sheep, yet their increase was slow, as the country abounded in wolves. It was therefore the work of time to secure a supply of wool. Deerskin was a substitute for cloth for men and boys, but not for women and girls, although they were sometimes compelled to resort to it. The women had to spin and generally to weave all the cloth for their families; and when the wife was feeble, and had a large family, her utmost efforts could not enable her to provide them with anything like comfortable clothing. The wonder is—and I shall never cease to wonder—that they did not sink under their burdens."

"An immense throng of passengers and travellers is passing into and out of Pittsburgh daily, during the warm season. Five or six steamboats arrive and as many depart daily, either for nearer or more distant ports: and the number of canal-boats it would not be easy to estimate. To accommodate these travellers, the city contains some of the best hotels in the country—in the world. The Monongahela House, itself a princely palace, is also a perfect model as regards its management. It stands near the end of the Monongahela bridge, opposite the steamboat landing; and from its balconies and the beautiful terraces on the top, the traveller may view the city, the rivers, with the surrounding scenery, and the arrival and departure of steamboats. It was commenced in 1840, and finished in 1841. It is five stories high, with a front towards the river of 120 feet, and 160 feet on Smithfield Street; and with the ground cost about $100,000. It is kept by Mr. James Crossan. The Exchange Hotel, surpassed in splendor only by the Monongahela House, is kept by Messrs. Smith and M'Kibbin, on the same orderly and correct system that gave it its original celebrity under Mr. Crossan. The other hotels of the city are also highly respectable."

"Pottsville, like all the other towns in the coal region, is of recent origin. Previous to 1824 there was scarcely a dwelling on the spot where the town now stands. The excitement which followed the discovery of coal, brought to the place a swarm of adven-

turous spirits, which rendered it the focus of unprecedented speculations in coal lands and town lots.
In the midst of this excitement, the town took a run-
and-jump into existence. It never went through the
slow and gradual movements of a baby-existence;
but with one tremendous bound, found itself nest-
ling at the foot of a high mountain, swarming with
hungry speculators and eager adventurers of every
description—young, old, and ugly—green, black,
and brown—all huddled together and 'Eager for
the Fray.'

"The late Joseph C. Neal, who was one of the motley mass, some years afterwards, wrote the following humorous description of the speculating scenes:

" 'In the memorable years to which we allude,
rumors of fortunes made at a blow, and competency
secured by a turn of the fingers, came whispering
down the Schuylkill and penetrating the city. The
ball gathered strength by rolling, young and old
were smitten with the desire to march upon the new
Peru, rout the aborigines, and sate themselves with
wealth. They had merely to go, and play the game
boldly, to secure their utmost desire. Rumor declared
that Pipkins was worth millions, made in a few
months, although he had not a sixpence to begin
with, or to keep grim want from dancing in his
pocket. Fortune kept her court in the mountains of
Schuylkill county, and all who paid their respects to

her in person, found her as kind as their wildest hopes could imagine.

" 'The Ridge-road was well travelled. Reading stared to see the lengthened columns of emigration, and her astonished inhabitants looked with wonder upon the groaning stage-coaches, the hundreds of horsemen, and the thousands of footmen, who streamed through that ancient and respectable borough, and as for Ultima Thule, Orwigsburg, it has not recovered from its fright to this day!

" 'Eight miles further brought the army to the land of milk and honey, and then the sport began— the town was far from large enough to accommodate the new accessions; but they did not come for comfort—they did not come to stay. They were to be among the mountains, like Sinbad in the valley of diamonds, just long enough to transform themselves from the likeness of Peter the moneyless into that of a Millionaire; and then they intended to wing their flight to the perfumed saloons of metropolitan wealth and fashion. What though they slept in layers on the sanded floors of Troutman's and Shoemaker's bar rooms, and learned to regard it as a favor that they were allowed the accommodation of a roof by paying roundly for it, a few months would pass, and then Aladdin, with the Genius of the Lamp, could not raise a palace or a banquet with more speed than they!

" 'One branch of the adventurers betook themselves to land speculations, and another to the slower process of mining. With the first, mountains, rocks, and valleys changed hands with astonishing rapidity. That which was worth only hundreds in the morning, sold for thousands in the evening, and would command tens of thousands by sunrise, in paper money of that description known among the facetious as slow notes. Days and nights were consumed in surveys and chaffering. There was not a man who did not speak like a Croesus, even your ragged rascal could talk of his hundreds of thousands.

" 'The tracts of land, in passing through so many hands, became subdivided, and that brought on another act in the drama of speculation: the manufacture of towns, and the selling of town lots. Every speculator had his town laid out, and many of them had scores of towns. They were, to be sure, located in the pathless forests; but the future Broadways and Pall Malls were marked upon the trees; and it was anticipated that the time was not far distant when the deers, bears and wild-cats would be obliged to give place and take the gutter side of the belles and beaux of the new cities. How beautifully the towns yet unborn looked upon paper! the embryo squares, flaunting in pink and yellow, like a tulip show at Amsterdam; and the broad streets intersecting each other at right angles, in imitation of the common parent, Philadelphia. The skill of the artist was exerted to render them attractive; and the more German text, and the more pink and yellow, the more valuable became the town! The value of a lot, bedaubed with vermillion, was incalculable, and even a sky parlor location, one edge of which rested upon the side of a perpendicular mountain, the lot running back into the air a hundred feet or so from the level of the earth, by the aid of the paint box, was no despicable bargain: and the corners of Chestnut and Chatham Streets, in the town of Caledonia, situated in the centre of an almost impervious laurel swamp, brought a high price in market, for it was illustrated by a patch of yellow ochre!

" 'The bar-rooms were hung round with these brilliant fancy sketches; every man had a roll of inchoate towns in the side-pocket of his fustian jacket. The most populous country in the world is not so thickly studded with settlements as the coal region was to be.' "